D1240536

~∾⊙∽PASSAGES∾⊙∽~

Handfasting

A PAGAN GUIDE TO *Commitment Rituals*

Rev. Dr. Kendra Vaughan Hovey
Series Editor: Arin Murphy-Hiscock

PROVENANCE
PRESS

Avon, Massachusetts

Copyright © 2008 by F+W Publications, Inc.

All rights reserved.
This book, or parts thereof, may not be reproduced in any
form without permission from the publisher; exceptions
are made for brief excerpts used in published reviews.

The Provenance Press® name and logo design are
registered trademarks of F+W Publications, Inc.

Published by Adams Media, an F+W Publications Company
57 Littlefield Street
Avon, MA 02322
www.adamsmedia.com

ISBN-10: 1-59869-447-2
ISBN-13: 978-1-59869-447-5

Printed in Canada.
J I H G F E D C B A

Library of Congress Cataloging-in-Publication Data
Hovey, Kendra Vaughan.
Passages : handfasting / Kendra Vaughan Hovey and
Arin Murphy-Hiscock.
p.   cm.
ISBN-13: 978-1-59869-447-5 (pbk.)
ISBN-10: 1-59869-447-2 (pbk.)
1. Marriage customs and rites. 2. Marriage—Religious
aspects—Neopaganism. 3. Marriage—Religious aspects—
Goddess religion. I. Murphy-Hiscock, Arin. II. Title.
GT2690.H68 2007
392.5—dc22   2007015754

This publication is designed to provide accurate and authoritative information with regard to the subject matter covered. It is sold with the understanding that the publisher is not engaged in rendering legal, accounting, or other
professional advice. If legal advice or other expert assistance is required, the
services of a competent professional person should be sought.

—From a *Declaration of Principles* jointly adopted
by a Committee of the American Bar Association
and a Committee of Publishers and Associations

Many of the designations used by manufacturers and sellers to distinguish
their product are claimed as trademarks. Where those designations appear
in this book and Adams Media was aware of a trademark claim, the designations have been printed with initial capital letters.

This book is available at quantity discounts for bulk purchases.
For information, please call 1-800-289-0963.

To my husband Timothy,
my soul mate,
whom I love more and more each new day.

CONTENTS

SERIES EDITOR'S INTRODUCTION
Arin Murphy-Hiscock

THROUGHOUT LIFE we experience transitions and transformations that we wish to mark in some way, in order to highlight them and celebrate their importance both to us and to others. Rites of passage focus on these major shifts and transitions in life, and serve to allow both the individual involved and the surrounding community to celebrate them. A rite of passage is literally a rite wherein one explores the transition from one state to another. All too often today a rite of passage is limited only to the aspect of celebration, and we forget that meaning can be found through simple and careful consideration of the change in which we find ourselves absorbed.

Marriage is one of these momentous events, a day of great joy for two individuals as they vow to share their lives. This joy is shared by their families and friends, who lend their love and honor to the magnitude of the vow by witnessing it.

Handfasting is the joining of hearts and spirits before the Gods or human witnesses, a deep commitment that is not necessarily defined by legal status. The name arises from the handshake used to seal the vow, or the custom of binding the hands of the partners together to symbolize the new single partnership created by the vow of two individuals. Various forms of union based on this custom have been used in different cultures through the ages. The custom is seen in some as spiritual, in others as secular. Handfasting could be temporary for a defined period of time, be considered an engagement, or be a permanent matter.

Today, the term *handfasting* is generally used to denote a Neo-Pagan wedding, and commonly includes some form of the physical binding of the hands of the individuals being joined. Like its antecedents it can be permanent or temporary, but it is primarily considered to be a spiritual union. Fortunately, modern handfastings can also be legally binding unions if performed by a recognized and registered officiant.

Weddings performed in established mainstream religions have the benefit of a body of lore, philosophy, and tenets to support them, and thus a couple understands exactly what the spiritual aspect of marriage is within their religious structure of choice. Neo-Paganism faces the challenge of being an aggregate of loosely defined earth-based spiritual paths with wide-ranging beliefs and practices, often based on the personal experience of the individual following the spiritual path. There is no defined spiritual context for marriage within such an aggregate, and therefore those seeking to be married within the Neo-Pagan structure are faced with identifying their own spiritual expectations and context for the transformative rite of marriage. This can be a daunting task, for it requires two people to engage in profound self-examination in order to define a part of the greater mystery that lies at the heart of the Neo-Pagan spiritual path: the meaning of love, the presence of the Divine in one's life, and the sacred connection to the energy of life itself.

Handfasting: A Pagan Guide to Commitment Rituals presents such an examination of the spirituality of marriage from a Neo-Pagan point of view. It explores the historical and cultural sources of this ritual, as well as investigating the spiritual well-being and expectations of both individuals seeking to be united, illustrating the challenges that must be met in order for the marriage to succeed on a spiritual level. One of the associated themes of this book is the challenge of interfaith marriage. When the two individuals share the same faith, they can offer one another spiritual support and share in religious celebration. Interfaith relationships can be more challenging. The spiritual support shared by a same-faith couple must be defined in a different way for an interfaith partnership, which requires courage and strength to succeed.

This book explores the spiritual aspect of handfasting, and the secular and spiritual consequences of choosing this form of union. It also offers practical advice on how to plan a Neo-Pagan wedding, from choosing an officiant to planning the food, with special focus on creating meaningful ritual using spiritual symbolism. Reverend Dr. Kendra Vaughan Hovey's approach to this topic is very contemporary, based in healthy love and respect for the self as well as love and respect for a partner, while honoring the roots of the handfasting tradition and respecting what makes it so loved by Neo-Pagans. Reverend Dr. Kendra, founder and spiritual leader of the First

Church of Wicca, has officiated several Pagan and interfaith marriages, and has counseled partners through challenges in their married lives. Her sensitivity and insight into the unique needs of a Neo-Pagan handfasted union make her an excellent guide through the challenges of creating a wedding day that is personally meaningful and also practical.

Let this book inspire you as you plan your wedding, whether it be a ceremonial handfasting, a private handfasting witnessed only by the Gods, or a full formal wedding drawing on the traditions of both an established religion and your chosen Neo-Pagan path. May your memories of this portion of your spiritual journey be joyful.

Imbolc 2007

ACKNOWLEDGMENTS

Thanks to the God and Goddess for choosing me to do Your work.

Thanks to Adams Media, especially Andrea Norville, for approaching me about writing this book and for answering my endless e-mails, and to Katrina Schroeder for managing this project.

Thanks to Arin Murphy-Hiscock for offering your support and for writing the preface.

Thanks to my husband Timothy and my children, Alec and Alana, for your excitement, enthusiasm, understanding, constant support, and much-needed help.

Thanks to my congregation for giving me the time and understanding that I needed to complete this project.

Thanks to John Doonan for your help with the incense recipes.

Last but not least, thanks to Bruce Barrett for your unprecedented editing skills. I could not have done it without you!

The word handfasting *derives from the
wedding custom of tying the bride and
groom's hands or wrists together.*

CHAPTER 1

HISTORY AND ORIGIN OF
HANDFASTING CEREMONIES

EXPERTS DISAGREE ON the origin of handfasting. Some Neo-Pagans insist that the handfasting tradition can be proven to date back to ancient Paganism. Others say that handfasting can be traced back to pre-biblical times, but that there is no solid evidence suggesting that it was a Pagan tradition at all. One thing is certain: modern Pagans, and especially Wiccans, use the handfasting ritual for everything from declaring mutual romantic love to expressing legally recognized marriage vows.

Understanding handfasting requires that we understand the concept of marriage in Scotland starting from pre-biblical times. It was necessary then for anyone who was to marry to have the consent of their parents. More importantly, the marriage was not considered binding until it was consummated. Often young children would declare their love for one another, or be betrothed by their parents, with an agreement to marry in the future. This was considered a legal contract between the two and would prevent either of them from marrying anyone else. This vow of future commitment can be compared to that of the modern day engagement ring, which is a conditional gift. It is not legal in the United States for a woman to keep her engagement ring today unless she makes good on the promise to marry. If the marriage ends in divorce, it is acceptable that the ex-wife keeps her ring under the grounds that she fulfilled her commitment to marry.

The Christian Church, in the late Middle Ages, taught that even if two people ran off together against their parents' wishes, this would still constitute a legal marriage. In fact, the Christian Church didn't even require that the couple consummate the marriage for it to be legally binding. The "consented marriage" was considered a legal union from around the 1200s until the Protestant Reformation in the 1500s. It was common in Scotland and England to be married on the porch of the church (being married inside the church was only for the affluent). Of course, there were many couples that did not want to be married the traditional way, for many of the same reasons that couples elope today. The most important factor that bound two people in marriage was mutual consent.

Many couples would perform marriage on their own, knowing that their vows wouldn't be recognized by both church and state. Often, they chose this option because they could avoid uncomfortable conflict if someone did not approve of the marriage, because it was a cheaper option than a church wedding, or because it could be performed on a whim. These "secretive" marriages, performed alone on a hillside in the country, were no less marriages from a civil perspective than the ones that were performed on the porch of the church. Also, unlike today, if a couple were married in the late Middle Ages they were considered married for life in Roman Catholic Europe. The only thing that could break a binding marriage was death. It wasn't until the 1500s in Scotland and England that divorce and remarriage even became a possibility under canon law.

Although the Catholic Church and some emerging Protestant churches preferred a "proper" church wedding during medieval times, consisting of a formal ceremony with witnesses led by clergy in order for a couple to be recognized by the church, the civil laws recognizing personal, private vows remained in effect until 1939. In the late Middle Ages in Scotland and Northern England, the term *handfasting* was used to describe the mutual commitment ceremonies discussed above, and also commonly referred to agreements to marry in the future. These agreements bound the two people together in the eyes of the church and the state, and prevented them from handfasting or marrying another. The interesting fact here is that the handfasting was used more as a promise between two people, often minors, to declare their love for one another and a promise to marry at some point in the future. These declarations were considered completely binding by both the church and the state. If the couple consummated the marriage, then they were no longer considered "engaged." They were married.

By the late 1700s in Europe, handfasting ceremonies were no longer practiced as a common form of engagement. Instead, in Ireland from the 1700s through the early 1900s, there are several documented cases of handfasting being used as a trial marriage. Men would choose their wives on a trial basis by engaging in handfasting rituals. The couple would live together, engage in sex, and act as a married couple for a trial period of a year and a day. When that time was finished, if the couple had no children, they could choose to part ways, free to find new partners. Or they could call for a priest to marry them permanently.

The word *handfasting* derives from the wedding custom of tying the bride and groom's hands or wrists together. The hands were bound with a cloth or specially designed cord as part of the ceremony or ritual. In some ceremonies, the cord was not untied until the marriage was physically consummated. The term itself comes from the Anglo-Saxon word *handfaestung*, which was a custom of shaking hands over a contract. This was often the contract entered into when a man made a down payment, or *wed*, to his future wife's father in order to have her hand in marriage. This was the origin of the modern word *wedding*.

The Irish maintained an ancient tradition until the nineteenth century in which men and women would gather on opposite sides of a high wall, men on the North side and women on the South. The women would put their hands through holes in the wall and the men would pick one of the hands. The pairs thus formed would then live together for a year and a day. After that period of time they would decide whether or not they wanted to enter into permanent marriage. Interestingly enough, this festival took place on Lughnassad, a Sabbat celebrated on August 2nd by Neo-Pagans. By the late 1900s, this concept of handfasting as an ancient Celtic practice became well established and accepted. Several Neo-Pagan faiths have adapted the concept of ancient handfasting, and added their own beliefs and practices to the ritual. Some examples of ancient and new traditions used in modern handfasting ceremonies are:

+ The renewal of handfasting vows several times without the permanency of marriage
+ Stating in the handfasting vows that the bond lasts only as long as the two shall love one another
+ The handfasting ribbon or cord ceremony where the couple hold hands, right hand to right hand and left hand to left hand, and then intertwine a cord or ribbon in the infinity sign, knotting it three times
+ Keeping the handfasting cord bound until the union is consummated
+ Keeping the handfasting cord bound until the ritual is over
+ Using a handfasting as a religiously recognized but state-unrecognized marriage
+ Performing a handfasting ritual with an ordained cleric so it is a state-recognized marriage, incorporating a "legal" handfasting with an exchange of wedding rings

Thus, the history of handfasting is not entirely clear. One cannot prove that it was primarily a Pagan practice, nor trace its precise roots. Today handfasting is clearly a Pagan practice, and especially Wiccan. Like many Wiccan rituals, handfasting can be celebrated in a multitude of ways to fit the couple's particular Wiccan tradition. In later chapters different types of handfasting ceremonies are explored, with tips on how to prepare and throw the perfect handfasting for you and your partner.

*If you are looking for the strength to
ensure that no matter what happens
in your union you will not give up,
Demeter is the Goddess to invoke.*

CHAPTER 2

GODS AND GODDESSES

INVOKING GODS AND GODDESSES during your handfasting ceremony is a Neo-Pagan practice that ensures your union will be blessed with Their divine qualities. There are Gods and Goddesses from many different pantheons in mythology who may be invoked during your handfasting. A pantheon is a collection of divine beings gathered by a particular people or religion. All have Their own captivating stories. Whether you believe that the stories are true or are just ancient folklore developed over time to be used as a type of fable, the impressions these stories leave in your mind can be inspirational.

Metaphysics teaches us to look beyond the factual meanings of mythological stories. You learn from your own thoughts and impressions as they are stirred by the stories, resonating with ideas and experiences found in your subconscious mind. *You* interpret the lessons these stories teach. *You* learn how they can be related to your own life. The beauty of metaphysics is that there is no single correct interpretation for any of these stories. Indeed, your own interpretation, as it relates to your personal life, can change as time passes.

Below you'll find the names of some wonderful Goddesses and Gods from different pantheons as well as what they are best known for, and how you can use this knowledge when deciding which Goddess and God to invoke for your handfasting ritual.

I encourage you to do more research on your own and to see if the purpose suggested for each Goddess and God works for you. It is important to be certain that you have chosen the correct ones for this life-altering day. Do the research and, above all, trust your intuition in making the proper decision.

Know that it is *not necessary* to choose one of these specific traditional Gods or Goddesses. You may be more comfortable just invoking the "God and Goddess" or the "Lord and Lady." That is fine, as long as your invocation expresses what you are asking from Them. Please do not mix pantheons. If you pick a Greek Goddess, stick with a Greek God. It is disrespectful to cross pantheons. Most of all—just have fun!

Aztec Goddesses

∞ Chalchiuhtlicue ∞

She is the Aztec Goddess of the oceans, rivers, and running water. She is also the protector of women in labor and the patroness of childbirth.

Metaphysical Interpretation   Anything that rules over water rules over your emotions.

Use in Handfasting If you or your partner is overly emotional, you might invoke this Goddess for Her compassion and love. Also, She would be a great Goddess to ensure ease in labor and delivery, if you and your partner are planning to have children.

∞ Chicomecoatl ∞

She is a Goddess of food and vegetables, but especially corn. Thus, She is the Goddess of fertility.

Metaphysical Interpretation Corn is one of the best-known symbols of fertility and abundance.

Use in Handfasting She is the Goddess to invoke if you are looking for spiritual growth in your union, or if you want a large family.

∞ Ichpuchtli ∞

She is a Goddess of love, marriage, fertility, and sex. The marigold is Her sacred flower.

Metaphysical Interpretation Witches have always believed that the marigold is the flower of the sun and symbolizes passion and creativity. It has also been used by witches to bring softer words from a harsh tongue, and to assist a couple in talking with one another instead of arguing with one another.

Use in Handfasting Invoke this Goddess if you and your partner tend to have very heated arguments. She will aid you and help ensure that you learn to communicate with one another more effectively.

∞ Mama Pacha ∞

She is a fertility Goddess sometimes portrayed as a dragon. She rules over plantings and harvesting. Some believe She is the cause of earthquakes.

Metaphysical Interpretation　Sometimes when we are in a relationship for a long time, things can tend to get very routine, stagnant, and boring.

Use in Handfasting　Invoking this Goddess will ensure that things get a little exciting for you, and remind you why the two of you fell in love in the first place.

∞ Tlazolteotl ∞

She is a Goddess of sex and childbirth. The name *eater of filth* was given to Her because She visits people on their deathbed. She allows people to confess their sins to Her, and then She would eats the sins.

Metaphysical Interpretation　We all have skeletons in our closet, things we have done in our past that we are embarrassed about or want to forget. More often than not, we have never shared these things with anyone else, so they fester inside, and can cause us to sabotage our own happiness.

Use in Handfasting　Invoke this Goddess when you want to release baggage from the past so that you can move forward.

∞ Xochiquetzal ∞

She is a Goddess of pregnant women, fertility, and flowers. She is often portrayed enveloped in birds and butterflies.

Metaphysical Interpretation   Birds and butterflies symbolize new beginnings. This could be the new beginning of your relationship, or the children that you will create together.

Use in Handfasting   Invoke this Goddess when you want to embrace the newness and the innocence of your love.

Aztec Gods

∞ Eueucoyotl ∞

He is a God of freedom, fun, sex, and spontaneity.

Metaphysical Interpretation   We can all get stuck in a rut. Sometimes we feel that we have gotten into a routine in life that is constant, never-changing, and predictable.

Use in Handfasting   Invoke this God when you want to add some spark to your life. If you are the type of person who gets stuck in the routine of life, this God will ensure that you remember to have fun, too.

∞ Quetzalcoatl ∞

He is a God of wind, and thus brings the breath of life. He is a God who is forever tempted by demons to commit murder, but His feelings of love are too great to succumb. He is the most compassionate of all the Gods.

Metaphysical Interpretation With the wind comes a breath of fresh air, rejuvenation. You can really feel the presence of your Divine Being in a cool summer breeze. With that feeling comes serenity, love, and compassion.

Use in Handfasting Invoke this God when you or your partner need to be reminded that you are already one with the Universe, and it is okay to slow down and become one with Nature.

Canaanite Goddesses

∞ Asherali ∞

She is best known as a moon and fertility Goddess, or the Hebrew bread of life Goddess.

Metaphysical Interpretation Bread is produced from the grain that gives and sustains life. The moon is symbolic of our emotional needs in life. Asherali balances our emotional and physical needs.

Use in Handfasting Invoke this Goddess if you are looking for a balance between the *physical* and *spiritual* in your union.

∞ Astarte ∞

She is best known as a maiden Goddess of love and war. She is associated with the planet Venus and is a fertility Goddess.

Metaphysical Interpretation The polar opposites of harmony and conflict. Every relationship experiences these opposites. We can't expect to have a relationship and never disagree, but we can expect to have love and compassion for the opposing view.

Use in Handfasting Invoke this Goddess to ensure that opposing views are in balance and able to be seen with love, compassion, and understanding.

∞ Naamah ∞

She is best known as a Goddess of sex and love. She is also worshiped as the inventor of divination.

Metaphysical Interpretation Divination is a way to see into the future and also a way to see what you need to do in order to please others by giving of yourself.

Use in Handfasting Invoke this Goddess when you need to look into the future for guidance, and to learn new ways to please your partner.

Canaanite Gods

∞ El ∞

He is a God of mankind and is best known as the ruler of the desert, where He resides with His two wives and many children.

Metaphysical Interpretation   The desert is symbolic of hard times and limited resources, yet El is able to enjoy the bounty of prosperity and fertility with His many children.

Use in Handfasting   If you are looking for a God to ensure that all of your challenges in your union come out happy, you would want to invoke El.

∞ Mot ∞

He is a God of the dry season, death, and sterility.

Metaphysical Interpretation   This God symbolizes hard times and limited resources. This is a reminder that a loving union is not always perfect. Sometimes we want to run away, but the grass is not always greener on the other side.

Use in Handfasting   Invoke Mot if you and your partner do not want to have any children. Mot will ensure harmony in marriage without the need to procreate.

Celtic Goddesses

∞ Achtland ∞

The Goddess Achtland was originally a mortal woman best known for being dissatisfied with mortal men. She fell in love, though, with one of the Tuatha De Danaan (people of the Goddess Danu). When She married him and joined him in the land of the Sidhe, She, too, became immortal.

Metaphysical Interpretation Achtland was looking for a man who could challenge Her spiritual nature and intellect. She wanted more from a man than someone who would allow Her reckless behavior; She yearned for a connection to Her higher power and found such a man living in the world of Faeries.

Use in Handfasting Achtland would be a wonderful choice for someone who is having a difficult time with the idea of settling down. She would also be a great choice for someone with a sincere passion for the Faerie realm.

∞ Aine ∞

Aine is a Goddess of the moon and of human love. She is the ruler of agriculture, and thus reigns over the fertility of people, crops, and animals. Aine is immortal, but was thought by ancient Celts to like men, and often had sexual relations with them so that She could give birth to faerie children. She is best invoked on or around the summer solstice.

Metaphysical Interpretation Grain is a metaphor for new life. Held within the grain are the seeds to begin life anew. The moon is symbolic of our emotions and intuition. When we put the two together, we have compassion, love, spirituality, and new beginnings.

Use in Handfasting Invoking the Goddess Aine for your handfasting will ensure an open, loving communication that is overseen by Spirit. Aine can also ensure that you are blessed with children.

∞ Aiobhell ∞

The Goddess Aiobhell is known as a Goddess of Love, combined with sexuality. She is famous for holding a midnight court to ensure that men are satisfying their wives sexually.

Metaphysical Interpretation   The act of sexual union can be one of the most spiritually uplifting experiences a person can have. There is no room for men to be selfish when it comes to the loving union of two spiritual souls. Aiobhell is the Goddess of sexual equality.

Use in Handfasting   Aiobhell would be a wonderful choice if you have not yet had sexual intercourse with your partner. She would ensure that your partner was loving, gentle, and selfless with you. What a beautiful way to begin your union with one another!

∞ Branwen ∞

Branwen is a Goddess of love and beauty. She is actually a daughter of the Welsh Sea God, Llyr. She married an Irish king in an effort to make peace between Ireland and Wales. Sadly, She was abused in that marriage.

Metaphysical Interpretation   Branwen teaches us that some people are attracted to only the physical attributes of another. It is very important that you think about why you are being handfasted. Be sure that you are not doing it for the wrong reasons. Also, be sure that you are not hoping that once the handfasting is over, your parents and your partner's parents will miraculously get along now that you are united.

Use in Handfasting   Invoke Branwen when you want Her to bring Her knowledge of past mistakes. Ask Her to look upon you to ensure that you are handfasting for the right reasons.

∞ Brigid ∞

Brigid is a triple Goddess, best known as the protector of the home and the hearth. In honor of Her healing abilities, the original settlers of the Celtic lands would find wells to leave strips of rags. People would come to the wells and wet the rags in them in order to wash themselves or clean their wounds.

Metaphysical Interpretation   These Celtic wells symbolized the life-giving abilities of the womb. Wetting the rags in the wells for healing manifests a mother's need to nurture and care for her children.

Use in Handfasting   Call Brigid if you want to take care of your family and your home. She will ensure that you are nurturing, compassionate, and loving in every aspect of your union, from taking pride and care of your home to raising healthy, well-adjusted children.

∞ Cerridwen ∞

Cerridwen is a Goddess of fertility. She has a cauldron that She uses to make a magick potion that stews for a year and a day, and promises wisdom for its users.

Metaphysical Interpretation   The cauldron symbolizes new birth and life, while the potion symbolizes the need for intellectual and spiritual knowledge.

Use in Handfasting   Invoke the Goddess Cerridwen when you want to have children who are wise in both their intellect and their spirituality.

∞ Macha ∞

Macha, one of the great redheaded queens of Ireland, is extremely strong, courageous, and determined. When both of Her brothers died, She fought Her father's two brothers and killed them so that She could wear the crown and rule Ireland as Queen.

Metaphysical Interpretation   We all hear that redheads are feisty. I imagine that this story is the historical reason why people who know a redhead are quick to say "You know how redheads are." Determination and courage can certainly get you far in life.

Use in Handfasting   Invoke Macha if you are looking for strength, courage, and determination in your union. This is a great Goddess to invoke at a handfasting because we all know that the first year and a day is the most challenging.

∞ Medb ∞

She is a Goddess of sexuality by means of intoxication. Medb would get Her prospective mates drunk and then have them participate in a marriage ceremony. Her requirements for Her men were that they were fearless, compassionate, and without jealousy. She is sovereign in Her own right, not through marriage.

Metaphysical Interpretation We all want our mates to be "intoxicated" by us. We want them to remain enamored by the very thought and sight of us, and of course we want them to remain forever faithful. Sometimes we need to take a closer look at our own actions to determine if what we want is being demanded or if it is truly warranted.

Use in Handfasting Invoke Medb when you want a mate rich in lust, but only for you. Medb will also help you always think of new and creative ways to delight and capture your mate over and over again, and will support the independent sovereignty of women.

Celtic Gods

∞ Angus Og ∞

Angus Og is a Celtic God of youth, poetic inspiration, and love. He was known to have four birds that flew above His head. It is believed that the symbol "XXX" after a signature (symbolizing kisses) came from this God.

Metaphysical Interpretation Romance is the key here. We all want a mate who is romantic and free to express his or her feelings. Many of us want public displays of affection throughout the duration of our relationship.

Use in Handfasting   If you are looking for a relationship where you and your partner are free to express your affection, whether in private or in public, Angus Og is your God of choice. Love birds will flutter over you both, for all to see.

◊ Mabon ap Modron ◊

He is a Celtic God of the hunt and was stolen from His mother when He was three days old. His captors kept Him in the land of Annwn, otherwise known as the Otherworld of eternal youth, health, and abundance. Because of the time Mabon ap Modron spent in Annwn, He remained in His twenties forever.

Metaphysical Interpretation   We have all heard the expression "You are only as old as you feel," and this story shows us that. No matter what tragedies we have been through in life (even kidnapping) we can learn to come out of them seeing the positive, and so reap the benefits of the experience.

Use in Handfasting   Mabon ap Modron is the perfect God to call upon when you want to be able to get new perspectives on old things. If you or your mate hold grudges and has difficulty seeing the positive in misfortune, then this is the God you want to invoke for your handfasting to assist you.

◊ Cernunnos ◊

He is a Celtic God of love, strength, passion, sex, energy, fertility, and transformation. He is often seen accompanied by a ram-headed serpent and a stag while He carries bags of gold.

Metaphysical Interpretation   Cernunnos is the epitome of what we all look for in the masculine—in ourselves and in a mate. In fact, it is more than what we are looking for in a mate—it is also what we are looking for as the foundation of our relationship.

Use in Handfasting   Invoke this God if you want a strong, broad foundation as you embark on your new life together as a couple.

∾ Manannan ∾

He is a Celtic God of the ocean. He resides over the Other-world of eternal youth and wealth. It is said that He has a magick cauldron that can cause one to turn invisible from the mist that pours out from it. This invisibility prevents oncoming enemies from attacking.

Metaphysical Interpretation   Sometimes we just want time for ourselves for reflection and introspection—a chance to feel that we can process things and handle them with grace and ease instead of quickly reacting.

Use in Handfasting   If you or your significant other flies off the handle rather than assessing a situation for what it really is, you might want to invoke Manannan for help in that area.

Egyptian Goddesses

∞ Bastet ∞

This Goddess is most often depicted as a woman with a cat's head. She is a Goddess of the moon, fire, cats, the home, and pregnant women. She is known to have two sides to Her personality. With Her gentle and nurturing side, She protects the home and pregnant women. In Her vicious and aggressive aspect, She is a true fighter when in battle.

Metaphysical Interpretation   We all have the need sometimes to unleash and let go of the soft side of our personality to stand up for what we believe in.

Use in Handfasting   Invoke this Goddess if you are *too* likely to let things roll off your back. There might be a time when you don't want to merely keep the peace. Your viewpoint is important and should be heard.

∞ Hathor ∞

She is a Goddess of love and music. She is also known as the Deity of happiness and the protector of pregnant women.

Metaphysical Interpretation   When we are in love we live in harmony with the rhythms of our union. This union of harmony brings forth new life, and our united love can protect the new lives we have created.

Use in Handfasting   Invoke this Goddess to help ensure harmonious love and protection between you and your loved one.

∞ Isis ∞

A Goddess of magick, She is considered the restorer of life to those already dead. She is known as a shining example of a wife and mother, and that is why the ancient Egyptians loved Her so much.

Metaphysical Interpretation   Through the use of magick and positive intention we can bring new life to what is stale.

Use in Handfasting   Invoke this Goddess if you want to bring magick in the form of new ideas and fresh perspectives to your relationship.

∞ Mut ∞

She is a mother Goddess; Her name actually translates to "mother." She was born to no one, one of the few Goddesses that gave birth to Herself.

Metaphysical Interpretation   When we turn inward during times of difficulty, we can reach a place of self-reflection and introspection, and so nurture ourselves.

Use in Handfasting   Invoke this Goddess to remind you to take time for yourself to reflect on the future of your relationship.

∞ Qetesh ∞

She is a Goddess of nature, sacred ecstasy, and sexual pleasure. In Her hands She carries a snake and a lotus flower, symbols of sex and fertility.

Metaphysical Interpretation We all have the need to feel loved and secure with our significant other in order to free ourselves emotionally and sexually. Letting go allows us to experience a deep spiritual connection that can be had no other way.

Use in Handfasting If you have a difficult time letting go sexually with your partner, this is the Goddess you should invoke.

∞ Taueret ∞

She is a Goddess of pregnant women and childbirth. She often assisted in the birth chamber during childbirth.

Metaphysical Interpretation New life and new beginnings are difficult and challenging. It is helpful if we can connect with our spirituality at this time of flux in order to ensure that we are not alone.

Use in Handfasting Invoke this Goddess when you are feeling overwhelmed and alone, but confident about your partner and your decision to handfast.

Egyptian Gods

∞ Amon ∞

He is the King of the Gods and very popular among the ancient Egyptian people because He protects the weak from the strong. He also ensures justice.

Metaphysical Interpretation   When we enter into a union with another, we want to protect our loved one from harm from anyone, no matter how powerful and dangerous. When we make the commitment to handfast, we are ensuring that, no matter what, we will always stand by our partner's side.

Use in Handfasting   Invoke this God if you want to ensure that you will have the strength and willpower to stand up for your partner in his or her time of need.

∞ Min ∞

He is a God of male fertility and rain. He is thought to give sexual powers to men.

Metaphysical Interpretation   The sexual power this God gives to men is the ability to father children. In mythological stories, rain symbolizes the life-giving bodily fluid called semen.

Use in Handfasting   Invoke this God if you want to have several children.

∞ Osiris ∞

He is the God of the earth and vegetation. He is responsible for the yearly drought and the flooding along the Nile river.

Metaphysical Interpretation   When we get passionate, our energy increases until we experience an outpouring of emotion. Once we have this spilling over, we need quiet time to recuperate in order to feed our passion once again.

Use in Handfasting   If you are looking for a relationship filled with the normalcy of life one moment, and then full of passion the next, invoke this God.

Greek Goddesses

∞ Antheia ∞

She is a Goddess of vegetation, gardens, blossoms, and human love. She is known to have worn flowery wreaths at parties and festivals.

Metaphysical Interpretation   Flowers symbolize romance for a woman. They tell a woman that she is being thought of, is loved, and will always be cared for.

Use in Handfasting   Invoke this goddess when you want to have a handfasting rich with flowers, and when you wear a tiara of flowers upon your head. She will ensure that your union is full of romance.

∞ Artemis ∞

She is a Goddess of nature, animals, women, and childbirth. In many parts of ancient Greece, before marriage, young girls would ceremoniously dedicate toys, dolls, and locks of hair to Artemis.

Metaphysical Interpretation   Artemis is symbolic of leaving childhood and moving on to adulthood, ready to take on adult responsibilities.

Use in Handfasting Invoke this Goddess if you are feeling insecure about leaving your childhood behind. She will ensure that you have a smooth transition.

∞ Astraea ∞

She is a Goddess of justice, and was the last of the Gods to live with mortal humans. She is also known today in the form of the constellation Virgo.

Metaphysical Interpretation We all want to be sure that when we are having difficulty and arguing with our partner, we can weigh each side of the story fairly and that justice will be served.

Use in Handfasting Invoke this Goddess if you have a difficult time allowing your partner to voice his or her opinion, and when it is difficult for you to listen to the other side without prejudgment.

∞ Demeter ∞

She is a Goddess who is named Mother Earth. She is known to preserve marriage and the sacred law. It is because of Demeter's tireless search for Her kidnapped daughter that we are blessed to experience the four seasons.

Metaphysical Interpretation When we see only sorrow and darkness, we need to be reminded that, if we search deep within to our divine connection, we will see the light—the path to enlightenment.

Use in Handfasting   If you are looking for the strength to ensure that no matter what happens in your union you will not give up, She is the Goddess to invoke.

∞ Hecate ∞

We now know Hecate as the Goddess of witchcraft, the underworld, and the crossroads, but She was originally known as the Goddess of the wilderness and the protector of childbirth. Hecate is often seen carrying a torch and a knife.

Metaphysical Interpretation   By Her torch we see light in the darkness—the path to new birth and enlightenment. She carries Her knife to cut the umbilical cord between the physical body and the spirit body at death.

Use in Handfasting   Invoke this Goddess if you have difficulty feeling grounded in the decisions you are making for your future. She will help you see the right way. Be very specific in what you ask of Her, because She may lead you to a place you were not prepared to go.

∞ Hera ∞

She is a Greek Goddess of love and marriage. She is the Queen of the Gods, and most often called upon by women who have unfaithful partners.

Metaphysical Interpretation   Sometimes we feel insecure about the commitments being made to us. This insecurity can stem from our own thinking, but sometimes it is warranted in fact.

Use in Handfasting   Invoke this Goddess when you want to ensure that your thinking and your actions do not sway your partner's or your intentions.

∞ Rhea ∞

She is considered the mother of the Greek Gods. She was known to have run away with Her sixth son Zeus in an attempt to save Him from being eaten by Cronus, the father of Zeus. When Cronus found Zeus, Rhea gave Him a stone to eat instead of Her baby, thus saving His life.

Metaphysical Interpretation   We need to be careful that the person we pick to spend the rest of our lives with will not cause us to have reason to run away and become deceitful in an attempt to save ourselves or our children.

Use in Handfasting   Invoke this Goddess to ensure that your relationship will not be abusive.

Greek Gods

∞ Anteros ∞

He is the winged God of mutual love. He was best known as the God who would punish people for not returning acts of love done upon them.

Metaphysical Interpretation   We always hear about people who are in a relationship and are unhappy because they are not being recognized for the hard work they put into it.

Use in Handfasting   Invoke this God when you want assurance that you will be appreciated for all that you do.

∞ Eros ∞

He was the ancient Greek God of love and sexual desire. He is known to harness the natural energy force we call love, and send it to humans. He is most often seen as a nude winged boy carrying a bow and arrows. He actually has two kinds of arrows. One causes love instantly, and the other causes total lack of interest.

Metaphysical Interpretation   When we are in love, it is as though we are suddenly struck by lightning, or an arrow. This love is true and everlasting, and sometimes we need to be reminded of that.

Use in Handfasting   Invoke this God when you want your union to be filled with that magickal moment of being struck with love over and over again.

∞ Hymen ∞

He was the God of wedding ceremonies and was known to attend weddings. If He did not, the marriage would not last.

Metaphysical Interpretation   We all want the Gods to bless our sacred day.

Use in Handfasting   Invoke this God when it is important to you that you feel a spiritual connection watching over you on this special day.

Norse Goddesses

∞ Freya ∞

She is the Goddess of love, beauty, and wealth. She had a cloak made of eagle feathers that allowed Her to change into a bird.

Metaphysical Interpretation   Sometimes we get caught up in the physical plane and forget that there is an equally important spiritual plane of existence. Being able to turn into a bird allows this Goddess the opportunity to visit that spiritual plane whenever She needs to.

Use in Handfasting   Invoke this Goddess when you want to be reminded throughout your union of the need to be rejoined with the spiritual plane of existence.

∞ Sif ∞

She is a fertility Goddess with long, corn-yellow hair representing ripe grain. She is said to symbolize the ideal woman.

Metaphysical Interpretation   We must always remember that looks aren't everything. While it is important that we are physically attracted to our partner, we must remember

that there is so much more to life than just that. We all grow
old.

Use in Handfasting   Invoke this Goddess when you want to
be reminded of all the reasons you chose your partner.

∞ Sjofn ∞

She is a Goddess of love and passion. The Norse people
believed that Her job was to stop fights between married
couples.

Metaphysical Interpretation   When we disagree, it can be
a healthy exchange of viewpoints and ideas, but when we
argue it turns into an unhealthy need to be right.

Use in Handfasting   Invoke Her when you want your differences of opinion to remain healthy throughout your union.

∞ Var ∞

She is a Goddess of love and marriage. She is best known as
the Goddess who would ensure justice to those who did not
keep their marriage vows.

Metaphysical Interpretation   Entering into a commitment
brings with it the promise to remain faithful, but sometimes
we are so worried about the commitment being made to *us*
that we cannot fully let ourselves go to experience true love.

Use in Handfasting   Invoke this Goddess if you are having a
difficult time trusting the vows that are being made to you.

She will carry the commitment in Her hands, and if there is a reason for concern, She will be sure to let you know.

Norse Gods

∞ Freyer ∞

He is a God of sensual love, fertility, and happiness. He has a sword that floats through the air.

Metaphysical Interpretation　The sword is a symbol of strength, honor, and protection. We all have times when we want our strength and honor to rise above all else with the ease of being weightless.

Use in Handfasting　Invoke this God when you want to show your loved one that you will honor and protect your loving union.

∞ Njord ∞

He is a God of fertile land and sailing. He is best known as the ruler of the winds and fire.

Metaphysical Interpretation　We all have times when we feel our passion rising from the flames within. The winds of love and life can shift and change continually.

Use in Handfasting　Invoke this God when you want to ensure that your marriage will not be turbulent with hurricane winds or tornadoes, so to speak, but your sexual unions will be.

Roman Goddesses

∞ Ceres ∞

She is a Goddess of agriculture and motherly love. She is best known for teaching humans how to grow grains and corn by nurturing the earth. She is one of very few Goddesses who spend time with humans daily.

Metaphysical Interpretation We all need spirituality and Deity involved in our daily lives in order to attain that balance between the spiritual and physical planes of existence.

Use in Handfasting Invoke this Goddess if you want a constant reminder of Deity in your life and that of your partner.

∞ Diana ∞

She is best known as a Goddess of the hunt and the moon. She is often seen with a stag and Her dogs.

Metaphysical Interpretation We all need to be reminded of our independence and our ability to ward off danger.

Use in Handfasting Invoke this Goddess if you and your partner tend to get too dependent on one another to the point that you can no longer recognize the need for personal space.

∞ Juno ∞

She is best known as a Goddess who oversees the human baby from birth through marriage. She is considered Queen of the Gods in Roman mythology. The month of June is named for Her, long the favorite time to marry.

Metaphysical Interpretation   When we are old enough to make a commitment to unite with another, it is time to let go of the old protection and come into new, unsheltered territory.

Use in Handfasting   Invoke this Goddess when you feel the need to have the old feelings of protection by your side one more time before embarking on the new.

∞ Maia ∞

She is an earth Goddess who is best known for midwifery. She is also known as the grandmother of magick because Her son, Hermes, is known as the inventor of magick.

Metaphysical Interpretation   It is an amazing miracle to see the birth of a child that has been created from the love of two people.

Use in Handfasting   Invoke this Goddess when you want to have children and ensure that their birth will be magickal.

∞ Vesta ∞

She is a Goddess of motherhood and domesticity.

Metaphysical Interpretation   We all wear many hats today and often find ourselves too busy to realize the importance of our role as a caregiver of the home.

Use in Handfasting   Invoke this Goddess when you want some guidance as to how to settle into the role of taking care of the home.

Roman Gods

∞ Cupid ∞

He is the Roman God of love and sexual desire. He is most often seen as a nude, winged boy carrying a bow and arrows. He shoots His arrows into humans, forcing them to fall in love. He is said to carry two sets of arrows: one that instills love and one that instills hatred.

Metaphysical Interpretation   When we are in love it is as though we are struck by lightning, or an arrow. This love is true and everlasting, and we need to be reminded of that.

Use in Handfasting   Invoke this God when you want your union to be filled with that magickal moment of being struck with love over and over again.

∞ Faunus ∞

He was known as a God of fertility. His dominion was the fields and the livestock.

Metaphysical Interpretation   New life sprouting from the old is an amazing gift from the Gods. It tells us that there is much to look forward to in life.

Use in Handfasting   Invoke this God when you want to ensure that you and your partner bring forth new life into this world.

In Wicca we worship the God and Goddess equally. There is no whole without the duality of the male and female, so be sure that you are invoking one God and one Goddess for your handfasting, and that They come from the same pantheon.

If you are a gay, lesbian, or a transgender couple, it is not necessary to choose your God and Goddess based on your "role" in the relationship. Keep in mind that in Wicca, equality of the Divine is of the utmost importance, so be sure to choose one God and one Goddess. All that is necessary is that you identify with the Deity in some way, whether through your feminine or your masculine side. Additionally, I would like to encourage heterosexual couples not to fall into the trap of the woman picking the Goddess and the man picking the God. Be sure that you both can identify with the Goddess and the God you select together.

*The real beginning of living Pagan lies
in establishing a relationship with the
God and Goddess. When you are in love,
you experience this relationship with the
God and Goddess firsthand, and thus
experience inner peace.*

CHAPTER 3

LOVE AND RELIGION

WHEN TWO PEOPLE fall in love, they share one of the most spiritually intense moments of their lives. Love is hard to define, but unmistakable when we feel it. Pagans add to this experience when they remember the saying "As above, so below."

Think about the meaning of those words. They speak to our relationship with the spiritual world and the physical world, the combination of universal and natural laws that apply to our inner and outer consciousness. "Inner consciousness" refers to the inner mind, the part of the mind that connects to Universal Spirit, or in our case, the God and Goddess. "Outer consciousness" refers to the physical realm and our physical limitations.

Metaphysically speaking, we know that everything in this universe, seen and unseen, known and unknown, is connected and thus a part of everything else. If you have previously established a relationship with the God and Goddess, you know exactly what I mean. If not, you may first experience this connectedness when you fall in 39 love. The phrase "as above" (the divine, the spiritual), "so below" (physical perception and action) will express each moment of your love as a sacred recognition—prayer, acclamation, command, and meditation all in one. As above, so below.

When you are in love, the physical world takes on a new meaning. Many things that would normally bother you become easy to cope with, solve, or ignore. It's as though they are just not important. Things that you have never especially noticed can become wonderfully important, to be cherished and savored. Things that you have always loved become splendid, and call you to share their splendor with your loved one.

Through the deep love you have for one another, you are able to live an existence that is fulfilling in the spiritual plane as well as the physical plane—the ultimate goal of living life as a Pagan. Living Pagan doesn't just mean taking care of the earth, appreciating nature in all of its glory, doing as ye will and harming none, or setting up an altar. The real beginning of living Pagan lies in establishing a relationship with the God and Goddess. When you are in love, you experience this relationship with the God and Goddess firsthand, and thus experience inner peace.

Take a few moments with your partner to experience and share your feelings. Below you'll find love meditations: one for you and your partner if he or she is Pagan, one for you and your partner if he or she is non-Pagan, and one for you alone if your partner is not open to meditation. These meditations will help you identify with the God and Goddess who reside within. As above, so below.

Pagan Couple Love Meditation

When the time comes, you can share extended spiritual moments as well. The following meditation is designed for a Pagan couple to share. Find a place where you will be undisturbed for at least one hour. I suggest that you set up your altar for this exercise.

YOU WILL NEED

A God candle (yellow or gold)
A Goddess candle (white or silver)
Candles for the four quarters (directions):
> *A green candle (North)   A red candle (South)*
> *A blue candle (East)   A purple candle (West)*

A small bowl of salt representing earth (North)
Incense (love or psychic) representing air (East)
Another red or orange candle representing fire (South)
A small bowl of water representing water (West)
Four red roses (one each for the God, the Goddess, you, and your partner)
A watch or clock with a sweep-second hand
A plate of crackers
A chalice or glass with water, grape juice, or wine

CLEANSE THE RITUAL AREA

Spend some time cleansing the space you will use—mentally brush away negativity to allow the positive to flourish. Have soft, soothing music in the background. This, too, will cleanse the area.

SET UP YOUR ALTAR

Place your God candle at the upper right-hand corner of your altar and the Goddess candle at the upper left. Place the four quarter candles at the edges of your altar representing the North, South, East, and West. If you are unsure of where the directions are in relation to your altar, use a compass. Now place the representations of the elements (earth, air, fire, and water) just inside the quarter candles. Light the incense and the candle representing fire. Place one of the roses next to the God candle and one of the roses next to the Goddess candle. Place the other two roses crisscrossed in the middle of the altar. You and your partner should kneel or sit in front of the altar facing each other. Take your time.

CAST THE CIRCLE

Choose which one of you will begin. Pick up the bowl with the water in it. Place three pinches of salt into the water bowl. Stand and walk *deosil* (clockwise, pronounced "jessil") around the perimeter of your circle, visualizing an intensely bright white light surrounding and protecting you and your loved one in your sacred space. Next, have your partner walk the perimeter of the circle (also *deosil*) with the incense, still visualizing the same intensely bright white light.

For the third time around the circle, one of you will take the God's rose (next to the God candle, representing the male principle). Starting at the South, walk *deosil* half of the way around the circle. The other will take the Goddess's rose. Starting at the North, walk *deosil* around the other half of the circle. Do this simultaneously, thus completing the third pass around the circle, each partner finishing half the circle. Face each other, and step forward to meet each other in the middle of the circle. Each of you finished the circle where the other began. This is done in an effort to show that you both will change. Learn to feel comfortable with it.

Now say together, "Our circle is cast. Together we have created sacred space. As above, so below."

CALL THE QUARTERS

Call the quarters together, to share with them the love you have for one another. Start at the North and call the quarters *deosil* (clockwise). It is customary to face the quarter that you are calling, and bow to the Spirits of the elements when you welcome them.

North

"We call to the North, Spirits of Earth, be with us as the foundation of learning about our relationship with each other and with the God and Goddess."

Light the green candle and say, *"Be with us. Welcome."*

East

"We call to the East, Spirits of Air, be with us with gentle words of love and compassion, as we learn more about each other and our relationship with the God and Goddess."

Light the blue candle and say, *"Be with us. Welcome."*

South

"We call to the South, Spirits of Fire, be with us as the passion of understanding for one another, and for the God and Goddess."

Light the red candle and say, *"Be with us. Welcome."*

West

"We call to the West, Spirits of Water, be with us, as emotions that run deep. Give us better understanding of each other and of the God and Goddess."

Light the purple candle and say, *"Be with us. Welcome."*

INVOKE THE GOD AND GODDESS

Next, you will need to invoke the God and Goddess. Choose who will invoke the God and who will invoke the Goddess. Also, instead of just using the words God and Goddess as suggested below, you may feel that you want to use the names of particular Deities, listed in Chapter 2. Be sure not to mix pantheons, because it is highly disrespectful. If you choose a Greek God, choose a Greek Goddess. When you invoke the God and Goddess it is customary to face the altar and bow to Them in respect when you welcome Them.

Invoking the God

"We call to the God, ruler of all that is courageous, committed, and strong. Be with us as we explore our love for each other and for You."

Light the God candle and say, *"Be with us. Welcome."*

Invoking the Goddess

"We call to the Goddess, ruler of all that is compassionate, nurturing, and patient. Be with us as we explore our love for each other and for You."

Light the Goddess candle and say, *"Be with us. Welcome."*

You are now ready to start your meditation. Take turns reading the following words right from this book to each other, using the second hand on your watch or clock to pay close attention to the pauses. Take turns reading the whole exercise, one reading to the other.

MEDITATION

"We are in love and I love you with all of my heart. I have been blessed by you in so many ways. My words are not enough to express my deep feelings of love, and gratitude that you have come into my life. You and I have many more things to explore and share together, but for now I would like you to take a few moments to just experience the deep feeling of love you have for me. Think about how our love feels. Feel it deep within your heart and soul. Let it consume your being for a few moments as you affirm and pray for yourself:

"'I deeply know the feeling of love. You are beautiful and I am blessed.'"

Pause briefly, and then repeat this affirmation for your partner: "I deeply know the feeling of love. You are beautiful and I am blessed."

Sit quietly as your partner meditates on these words for two minutes. When two minutes have passed, softly say, "When you feel your love for me the strongest, you know that the God and Goddess are manifesting Their love through you. You give me the gift of both your love and Theirs, but They have also given you a gift, the gift of Their unconditional love, which in turn gives you inner peace.

"I ask that you now affirm and pray, 'The God and Goddess love me unconditionally, and are my inner peace in all situations.'"

Slowly repeat this affirmation for your partner, "The God and Goddess love me unconditionally, and are my inner peace in all situations." Sit quietly as your partner meditates on these words for two minutes.

When two minutes are over softly say, "When I think about the love I have for you, I feel the exact same way you are feeling right now. It is our love for one another and our love for the God and Goddess that make all things possible. We can accomplish anything together—the four of us. Affirm and pray, 'All things are possible for us with the God and Goddess.'"

Repeat this affirmation for your partner, "All things are possible for us with the God and Goddess." Sit quietly as your partner meditates on these words for two minutes. When two minutes have passed, softly say, "I am thankful for the gift of true love and I will always remember what it feels like. The God and Goddess have blessed us with true love, and for this I give thanks. And so it is! Blessed be!"

Now ask your partner to gently open his or her eyes and come back to this space and time. Give your partner as long as he or she needs to ground and center, and then switch roles. Have your partner read the same meditation to you while you meditate.

CAKES AND ALE AND REFLECTION

When you are finished it is time for cakes and ale and reflection. Feed each other the crackers and the drink. Take some time to discuss what you experienced during your meditations. When did you feel most connected to each other? When did you feel most connected to the God and Goddess? Do you feel differently about each other now? Savor your experience together.

RELEASING THE CIRCLE

Now it is time to thank the God and Goddess, release the Spirits of the quarters, and release the circle. Be sure to face the altar when you release the God and Goddess and bow after you thank Them.

Thanking the Goddess

"Goddess, ruler of all that is compassionate, nurturing, and patient, we thank You for being with us as we learned more about our connection to each other and to You. Stay if You will, leave if You must. Blessed be!"

(You may extinguish the Goddess candle, or leave it lit until it goes out on its own.)

Thanking the God

"God, ruler of all that is courageous, committed, and strong, we thank You for being with us as we learned more about our connection to each other and to You. Stay if You will, leave if You must. Blessed be!"

(You may extinguish the God candle, or leave it lit until it goes out on its own.)

Now release the quarters. Start with the West because that is that last one you called. From there you want to release them *widdershins* (counterclockwise). Face the direction of the quarter as you release each one, and bow in respect once you have thanked them. Extinguish each candle as you release the associated quarter.

West

"Spirits of the West, of Water, thank you for being with us as emotions that run deep, and for giving us better understanding of each other, and of the God and Goddess. Stay if you will, leave if you must. Blessed be!"

South

"Spirits of the South, of Fire, thank you for being with us as the passion of understanding each other and the God and Goddess. Stay if you will, leave if you must. Blessed be!"

East

"Spirits of the East, of Air, thank you for being with us as the gentle words of love and compassion, as we learned more about our relationship with each other and the God and Goddess. Stay if you will, leave if you must. Blessed be!"

North

"Spirits of the North, of Earth, thank you for being with us as the foundation of learning about our relationship with each other, and with the God and Goddess. Stay if you will, leave if you must. Blessed be!"

Together, walk around the circle *widdershins* (counterclockwise). Visualize the bright white light dissipating around you as you walk and release the circle. When you have walked the perimeter of the circle, face the altar together. Hand each other one of the crisscrossed roses from the middle of the altar and say to each other in unison: "This circle is released, but never broken. Merry meet, merry part, and merry meet again!"

Sneak a kiss or hug, and feel free to speak your love. When you are ready, take the God and Goddess's roses and leave them somewhere special outside, as an offering. Your crisscrossed roses, you may keep as you wish. Do this meditation together as often as you like. It's a great way to reconnect with each other and with the Divine.

Interfaith Relationships

This all sounds so romantic and beautiful, but what happens when your partner isn't Pagan? One of the greatest things about being Pagan is your ability to accept the idea of free will and to use it responsibly. Free will means that we are free to choose the spiritual path that works for us as individuals. We also encourage others to find the paths that work for them. It is necessary, however, to be clear from the beginning that you will each be practicing different faiths, and that it is acceptable and comfortable for both of you.

In my own ministry, I have found that it is common for Pagans to have non-Pagan partners. Often the non-Pagan partner is very supportive of his loved one's faith, but will state clearly that it is not for him. The reverse is often true as well. A Pagan can be very supportive of his partner's choice of faith, or lack thereof, but also makes no bones about declaring that it is not for her, either. Fortunately, it is common today to see interfaith marriages based on acceptance. Diversity helps you acknowledge that you fell in love *because* you were so very different. An interfaith couple begins their union already knowing what it means to compromise and value one another's opinions, even if they differ. An interfaith couple has already agreed to disagree. This is the biggest step in a successful marriage.

Children are another consideration. All too often, couples come to me for counseling because they had decided before they got married that it was acceptable to practice different faiths, but never considered what it would mean when children came along. I've heard too many times that a Pagan partner agreed to have his child baptized in another faith because of the expectations of the extended family, but later felt devastated about it. The best advice I can give is this: an interfaith marriage is just that—interfaith. Neither religion is more important than the other. Look at the gift you can give your child by allowing her to be taught the foundations of both religions. A balance must be agreed upon and understood by both parents. It can be done. I urge you and your partner to discuss it now, not later.

Let's assume that your partner is understanding and tolerant of your religious choice and you of his. As a Pagan, you probably wish to feel more spiritually connected with your partner. Your partner's choice to follow another religion, or none at all, should not discourage you. Remember that we are all connected, whether your partner realizes it or not. There is no reason why you cannot feed him with your spirituality through the channel of the Universal Spirit or the God and Goddess. You needn't cast spells or alter your partner's free will, but you can send all of your love for him through the God and Goddess. They, in turn, will be sure that your partner gets it. On the flip side, every time that your partner loves you, whether or not he realizes it, he loves you from the place where the God and Goddess live within him. It's an amazing thing, and adds one more beautiful dimension to your whole relationship. I suggest that you embrace this beauty.

The following meditation is for an interfaith couple with a non-Pagan partner who is willing to meditate. In this case you will not use an altar or cast a circle. You must always respect your partner's choice not to practice the occult, but anyone of any religion may meditate.

Interfaith Couple Love Meditation

Choose a quiet room in your home where you can relax and the atmosphere feels spiritual. Play some quiet, relaxing music in the background, and ask your partner if it would be all right to light a candle. If your partner agrees, choose a red candle to represent love.

Sit on the floor facing each other and hold hands. Look into each other's eyes and affirm your love and respect for one another. It can sound something like this:

"I love you with all of my heart and I respect the decisions that you make for yourself because I know that you will also respect mine. Communication is the key to every healthy relationship and we are going to encourage that communication with this sharing exercise."

You will then say, "I am Pagan and I have love in my heart for you and the God and Goddess, and I honestly respect that you have different beliefs."

Ask your partner to share her beliefs with you, but do not try to change those beliefs. Just listen with an open heart and mind. Know that the God and Goddess are manifest through you, and that They hear your partner too. They will give you the strength to see beyond religion and to see pure love. Feel relaxed and comfortable, knowing that the God and Goddess are with you, and that your comfort is spilling over into your partner. Your partner will feel at ease, knowing that there is no tension between you, only love.

Ask your partner to close her eyes and to try and feel your deep love and affection through your mutual spiritual connection, and through the physical connection you share while holding hands. Let your partner know that you will concentrate on feeling the same from her. Silently affirm to the God and Goddess that you know They are helping you and your partner connect with this prayer: "God and Goddess, I thank You for helping my partner and me connect spiritually."

Now sit in the silence until you feel it has been long enough. When you have both opened your eyes, let your partner know how much you have appreciated her efforts, perhaps with a hug and a kiss. You can now sit quietly and reflect on what you both have experienced, but do not be discouraged or angry if your partner felt nothing. It was enough that that she was there.

Single-Person Pagan Love Meditation

The following meditation is for you alone if your partner is not able to share in meditation with you. If your partner refuses to meditate with you, this is not a precursor to a bad relationship unless you let it be. Respect your partner's wishes and he will respect yours. In a truly loving relationship, it is all right to disagree (and sometimes fun!).

PREPARING YOUR ALTAR
AND CASTING YOUR CIRCLE

If you have a home altar, use the list and instructions from the ritual above (page 41) to prepare your altar. Once your altar is decorated you will need to cast your circle. Pick up the bowl with the water in it, and place three pinches of salt into it.

Stand, and walk *deosil* (clockwise) around the perimeter of your circle, visualizing an intensely bright white light surrounding and protecting you in your sacred space. Next, walk *deosil* around the circle with the incense, visualizing the same white light surrounding and protecting you. For your third time around the circle, pick up both of the roses in the center of the altar, and walk *deosil* around the circle. When you have reached your starting point, place the roses back on your altar, crisscrossed.

Say, "I have cast my circle and created sacred space."

CALL THE QUARTERS

Call the quarters, and ask them to join you as you experience your love meditation. Show your respect to the quarters and the God and Goddess by bowing as described above (on page 43).

North

"I call to the North, Spirits of Earth, be with me as I learn to understand the foundation of my loving relationship with _____, and also with the God and Goddess."

Light the green candle and say, *"Be with me. Welcome."*

East

"I call to the East, Spirits of Air, be with me as the gentle words of love and compassion as I learn more about_____, and about the God and Goddess."

Light the blue candle and say, *"Be with me. Welcome."*

South

"I call to the South, Spirits of Fire, be with me as the passion of understanding for_____, and for the God and Goddess."

Light the red candle and say, *"Be with me. Welcome."*

West

"I call to the West, Spirits of Water, be with me as emotions that run deep. Show me better understanding of _____, and of the God and Goddess."

Light the purple candle and say, *"Be with me. Welcome."*

INVOKE THE GOD AND GODDESS

Next, invoke the God and Goddess. As above (page 44), you may use particular names for the God and Goddess, as long as you don't mix pantheons.

God

"I call to the God, ruler of all that is courageous, committed, and strong. Be with me as I explore my love for _____ and You."

Light the God candle and say, *"Be with me. Welcome."*

Goddess

"I call to the Goddess, ruler of all that is compassionate, nurturing, and patient. Be with me as I explore my love for _____ and You."

Light the Goddess candle and confidently say, *"Be with me. Welcome."*

You are now ready to start your meditation. I suggest that you use a tape recorder to record yourself reading the meditation and the timed pauses. You'll do this for two reasons: first, so that you can listen to your own words instead of reading them while trying to meditate; second, to avoid distracting time checks.

MEDITATION

"God and Goddess, as You already know I am in love with _____. My partner does not practice the same faith that I do. Although [he] [she] is supportive and tolerant of my religious choice and I am of [his] [hers], I would like to send my love, and Yours, combined, to [him] [her]. When You manifest through me, I will feel [his] [her] love equally as strongly as it unites with Your love for me."

Affirm and pray, "I feel intense love in the core of my being from both the God and Goddess and _____."

Repeat, "I feel intense love in the core of my being from both the God and Goddess and _____."

Allow two full minutes of silence (if recording, let your tape recorder run for the full two minutes).

Now softly say, "The feelings I have when I think of my partner can be so overwhelming. I want to share my love with [him] [her] and the rest of the world. I am blessed to be able to experience inner peace."

Affirm and pray, "You have given me the gift of knowing inner peace."

Repeat, "You have given me the gift of knowing inner peace."

Allow two full minutes of silence.

Now softly say, "When I think about the love I have for _____ I can internalize the love [he] [she] feels about me. It is our love for one another and my love for the God and Goddess that make all things possible. I can accomplish anything with _____ because I know You are always with us."

Affirm and pray, "All things in our life together are possible with You at our side."

Repeat, "All things in our life together are possible with You at our side."

Allow two full minutes of silence, and then softly say, "I am thankful for the gift of true love. I will always remember what it feels like. The God and Goddess have blessed me with true love. For this I give thanks. And so it is! Blessed be!"

RELEASING THE CIRCLE

Savor your meditation for as long as you wish. Enjoy the crackers and the drink. When you are finished, release the God and Goddess, the quarters, and the circle.

Goddess

"I thank You, Goddess, ruler of all that is compassionate, nurturing, and patient. Thank You for joining with me as I explored my love for _____ and for You."

Extinguish the Goddess candle and say, *"Stay if You will, leave if You must. Blessed be!"*

God

"I thank You, God, ruler of all that is committed and strong. Thank You for joining me as I explored my love for _____ and for You."

Extinguish the God candle and say, *"Stay if You will, leave if You must. Blessed be!"*

Now release the quarters *widdershins* (counterclockwise), in reverse order from your calling the quarters.

West

"Spirits of the West, of Water, of emotions that run deep. Thank you for giving me better understanding of _____, and of the God and Goddess."

Extinguish the purple candle and say, *"Stay if you will, go if you must. Blessed be!"*

South

"Spirits of the South, Spirits of Fire. Thank you for giving me the passion of understanding for _____, and for the God and Goddess."

Extinguish the red candle and say, *"Stay if You will, leave if You must. Blessed be!"*

East

"Spirits of the East, Spirits of Air. Thank you for joining me as gentle words of love and compassion as I learned more about _____, and about the God and Goddess."

Extinguish the blue candle and say, *"Stay if You will, leave if You must. Blessed be!"*

North

"Spirits of the North, Spirits of Earth. Thank you for joining me as I learn to understand the foundation of my loving relationship with _____, and also with the God and Goddess."

Extinguish the green candle and say, *"Stay if You will, leave if You must. Blessed be!"*

Now release the circle. Pick up the two crisscrossed roses, representing you and your partner, holding them gently together. Walk once around the circle *widdershins* (counterclockwise), visualizing that you are releasing the circle and that the bright white light dissipates around you as you go. When you have walked the perimeter of the circle, face the altar. Holding the crisscrossed roses, say softly, "This circle is released, but never broken. Blessed be!"

When next you see your partner, sneak a kiss or hug. Feel free to speak your love. Give him one of the roses, or keep them together in a place you both share. Take the God and Goddess's roses and leave them somewhere special outside as an offering. Do this solitary meditation as often as you like, to deepen your connection with your partner and with the Divine.

This chapter contained three combinations of love meditations and rituals and the blending of faiths within those relationships. Whichever dynamic you experience matters less than your solid relationships with the God and Goddess. Establish your relationship with the Divine, and then have faith that They will be with you and your partner every step of the way—no matter what!

Remember, too, that falling in love may be your sharpest, clearest experience of the beginning of your knowledge of the infinite love of the God and Goddess for one another, for Their creation, Their children, and for you. Love strips away the failures of religion, and leaves the brilliance of faith and of relationship.

In love, we find our prayer, our acclamation, and our hope: "As above, so below." In love, we find the Divine.

*Remember that your ceremony
is sacred to you and your loved
one, so there is no "right" or
"wrong" way to perform it.*

CHAPTER 4

HANDFASTINGS AND COMBINING TRADITIONS FOR MODERN WEDDINGS

NOW THAT YOU KNOW the history of handfasting, it is important to know about blending handfasting with other wedding traditions. Pagans have always believed in the supernatural, those unexplained forces that can prove to be a very positive influence in one's life, or at the other extreme, wreak havoc in the entire universe. Planted in the heart of this belief is an unquestioned truth that there are evil spirits "out there" that are lurking around, just looking for people to taunt and shower with misfortune. When two people unite, in the past or today, there is always a question as to whether or not the couple will find happiness, or be influenced by evil and thus doomed to misery. In pre-biblical times, when a couple joined in marriage, it was in the hands of the Gods to determine whether or not the couple would be eternally happy. Clearly, this line of thinking would offer those couples who were unhappy an explanation for their unhappiness: their union must be under attack by an evil spirit. Many ancient wedding traditions or customs have come down to us that were actually performed in order to prevent these 61 evil spirits from overtaking the couple as they embarked on their new life together.

Today, whether we practice these old traditions for the same superstitious reasons or because we feel that history is nostalgic and should be incorporated into our special day, we will find that some of these traditions have Pagan roots and some do not. Either way, many have been incorporated into the ceremonies of various faiths. As I explain these traditions, be sure to take some time in deciding which ones you would like to incorporate into your special day. This flexibility will allow you to customize *your* ceremony of union, and the spiritual frame of your life as a couple, therefore making it a modern tradition. Remember that your ceremony is sacred to you and your loved one, so there is no "right" or "wrong" way to perform it.

Today it is very uncommon to be of marriageable age and have been raised your whole life as a Neo-Pagan, so it would stand to reason that you would have practiced another faith before finding your way to Paganism. Thus, it is not uncommon for the Pagan partner to want to hold onto some of the old customs and traditions of her past religion. If this is true, then both partners should spend some time talking about which aspects of faith that they would each like to bring to the ceremony. It is very important that you both consider the discomfort either of you may have around this topic. Make sure that you ask the God and Goddess for guidance in reaching your compromises.

The big question here is "How do you and your partner really want the wedding to appear?" It would stand to reason that, if you want to incorporate both faiths and both families, you are not planning a simple handfasting, but a legal marriage that may incorporate a handfasting ceremony. So be sure to answer the following questions:

Do you want a Pagan wedding with undertones of another faith?

Do you want a wedding that is primarily another faith with Pagan undertones?

Do you want a nondenominational wedding with undertones of both faiths?

The latter is the easiest interfaith marriage ceremony to arrange, and is the least threatening to both parties and their families. Also, you do not have to struggle with the challenges of trying to find a minister or priest who will co-officiate such an arrangement with the Pagan partner's officiant. Admittedly, today you will find more weddings that are not only interfaith but combine different traditions quite nicely, to everyone's satisfaction. Spend some time reading over the traditions from various faiths in the next sections, and think about the ones that you and your partner might like to incorporate into your wedding. It is important that you are both happy on this day, one of the most important days of your lives.

European Pagan Traditions

There are several European Pagan traditions that can be incorporated into your handfasting ceremony. Below are some of the more common ones that you might want to incorporate into your special day.

Celtic Tradition

The Celtic tradition brings us the handfasting ribbon. In this ribbon or cord ceremony, the couple holds hands, right hand to right hand and left hand to left hand, and then the handfasting cord or ribbon is intertwined between them in the "infinity" sign. It is knotted three times at the bottom. The three knots in modern times symbolize the union of the couple intertwined with the Triple Goddess.

Throwing of rice, nuts, dried fruits, or sweets after the ceremony as the couple exits the church also came to us from ancient Celtic tradition. All of these foods were symbolic of fertility and happiness to be bestowed upon the new couple. Today, because of the environmental issues and concern for wildlife, it is more customary to throw paper confetti, as long as there is someone who is willing to immediately clean it up. Birdseed provides another common substitute.

Scottish Tradition

In the Scottish tradition, May was considered the most unlucky month to be wed. There is a popular saying that says "Marry in the month of May, and you will live to rue the day." May is the month in which the Sabbat Beltane is celebrated. Long ago, this festival was the time of year when young men and women paired off for lusty relationships without strings. Thus it was considered a poor time of year to begin a permanent relationship such as marriage. Additionally, it was bad luck to wed on a waning moon. This was sure to bring a decline in the love shared by the couple. June was considered a lucky time to marry because it was associated with Juno, the Roman Goddess of love and marriage. To this day, the majority of weddings take place during the month of June.

In the Scottish Pagan tradition it was customary for the bride to "walk with the sun" in the sanctuary where she was to be wed. She would first walk from East to West and then circle the church three times traveling *deosil* (clockwise or sunwise). This was done to prevent evil spirits from entering the ritual space and also to promote fertility. Today there are several ways to cast the circle for a handfasting ceremony. The options range from the bride to members of the handfasting party or, more commonly, the clergy casting it.

A Scottish custom that thankfully is never practiced today was to throw the wedding cake at the couple upon their honeymoon departure. This was done in an effort to ensure that the new couple would have a sweet happy life together. Today we still see the bride and groom feed each other the first servings of the cake, often with comical messiness reminiscent of the earlier "cake toss." A three-tiered cake for modern Pagans is considered good luck and symbolic of the Maiden-Mother-Crone.

Roman Tradition

The ancient Roman tradition brings us the veil. It was thought that brides were especially vulnerable to evil spirits, so Roman brides wore the veil in an effort to be unrecognizable, and so to trick these evil spirits away.

It was also customary in many traditions to carry the bride over the threshold. This would prevent her from coming into contact with any evil spirits who might steal her good luck, fertility, or vigor. The Romans had a different belief. They thought it was bad luck if the bride tripped over the threshold her first time through it, and so that is why she was carried. Of course, the groom could trip as well, but this wouldn't be so serious for the fortunes of the new household.

British Tradition

Although many historians trace the popular tradition of jumping the broom, or besom, to the slaves from West Africa, there is certainly enough evidence to suggest that it may in fact have been brought to us by the British Pagans. The besom has long been a symbol of fertility, stemming back to the Pagans who would jump over it in the fields where they had planted crops. It was said that the crop would grow as high as the person could jump over it with the besom. In the earthy symbolism of the ancients, the bristles of the besom represent the female genitalia, while the handle represents the male phallus. Together they represent the union of the male and female. It is customary at a modern Pagan handfasting to have the bride and groom jump over the besom.

There are two options for the ritual jumping. The first is to jump over it while it is held a few inches above the ground by the best man and maid of honor. The couple should jump over it as many times as the number of children they wish to have. The second is to lean the besom across the doorway of the couple's new home. They jump over it together to ensure good luck in the marriage. Of course, both methods may be used, since they represent different aspects of the couple's union. Most Pagan couples use the besom in a handfasting or a wedding ritual, jumping over it together at least once during the ceremony to ensure a happy and fertile marriage.

It is equally acceptable to jump over a cauldron instead of the besom. The cauldron has long been a symbol of fertility for witches, and was often associated with various Gods and Goddesses in the history of mythology. The cauldron can symbolize transformation, fertility, change, and new life—all good things to have in your new union.

Greek Tradition

Wedding rings come to us from the ancient Greek Pagans. Being round, the ring symbolizes the circle of life, the sun, the moon, and the earth. The ring clearly shows that there is no beginning and no end when it comes to true love. The Greeks believed that the vein of the ring finger on the left hand is the most direct route to the heart, and so a perfect place to wear a ring signifying love.

Throwing a bouquet of flowers is another tradition that dates back to ancient Greek times. We have all seen this practiced in modern weddings, where the bride stands with her back to all of the unwed women in attendance. She throws her bouquet of flowers over her head and into the crowd. The woman who catches it will be the next to wed. Today this tradition is paralleled by the groom throwing the bride's garter in the same fashion to the unwed men in attendance.

Turkish Tradition

Ancient Turks used a puzzle ring for their wedding ring. This is a ring in four parts that when put together looks like a typical ring with a lavish, knotted design on it. The groom would place the closed ring on the bride's finger. The bride was not shown how to put the ring back together if it were taken off. If the wife ever came home with it undone, the husband would know she had been unfaithful. After all, what bride could ever figure out how to weave a complex pattern back together once it had fallen apart? Turkish Pagans may have had a wise sense of humor about the risks of marriage, and you can imagine that Turkish grandmothers may have spent some giggling moments with their granddaughters explaining the complexities of weaving a marriage together with love, or weaving a ring together with skill and speed.

Christian Traditions

In the Catholic Church, it is customary to show devotion to Mary, the Mother of God. She is the ultimate role model for the Catholic bride. As a homemaker and future mother, the new wife will strive to have the same love for God and devotion to her family as Mary demonstrated. It is not uncommon for a Catholic bride to request a ritual during her wedding ceremony that includes the laying of flowers for the

Virgin Mary. However, these ceremonies are not a standard inclusion in the rite of marriage.

It is customary in the Christian faith to have a processional. The groom and the best man enter the church from a side door. Then the bride and groom's attendants escort one another up the aisle. Next, the maid of honor will walk up the aisle alone. Finally, the bride and her father walk up the aisle, and the ceremony proper begins.

Mexican Traditions

The tradition of the Lazo has been incorporated into the official marriage rite in Mexico and is celebrated by both Mexicans and Asians. The Lazo is a wedding rosary that is used to symbolize the joining of the couple through prayer. This rosary is made of two individual rosaries that join together as one near the crucifix. It is placed over the heads of the couple during the wedding ceremony to symbolize their spiritual union.

The giving of the Arras is also a Mexican tradition. The Arras is a small box that holds thirteen gold or silver coins. The coins represent Jesus and His Apostles. The groom gives the Arras as a gift to the bride after exchanging vows. This gift is a symbol of his intention and willingness to provide financial support to his family. In these more modern times, where two people often contribute financially to the household, this custom still reflects the religious intent of a united couple managing their finances together and prayerfully.

Jewish Traditions

It is customary for the bride and the groom not to see each other for a week before the wedding. The day of the wedding, just before the ceremony in a private room, the veil is placed over the bride's face by the groom. The veil symbolizes modesty, and the love of more than physical appearance.

The wedding ceremony takes place under a canopy called a chupah. The canopy symbolizes the home the bride and groom will now share. Usually, the bride and groom and both sets of parents meet under the canopy. It is also customary to walk around the canopy seven times before entering it. This symbolizes the seven days G-d (The "o" is removed because it is disrespectful in the Jewish faith to speak or spell the word. The word "Lord" is spoken in its place.) took to create the world that we live in.

It is customary in the Jewish faith that the wedding rings be made of solid gold, with no decorations or jewels. This symbolizes a union that is simple and beautiful in its own right. Jewels, with their imperfections, are symbolic of a marriage starting on the wrong foot. Additionally, in Jewish tradition the wedding ring is worn on the first finger of the right hand. At the conclusion of the ceremony the ring is generally moved to the left ring finger.

In the Jewish faith, it is customary to sign a marriage contract. This contract is called a *ketubah*. This marriage contract states that the groom will accept the responsibility of providing food, clothing, and shelter for his wife. Additionally, he agrees to be attentive to her emotional needs. Once signed, this contract is given to the bride for safekeeping and easy access.

It is customary to recite the seven blessings at the wedding of a Jewish couple. The seven blessings are usually recited by different chosen members of the bride and groom's families and friends. The first blessing is made over wine, and the person who reads this blessing drinks from the wine first. Then the groom drinks from the glass, and hands it to his future mother-in-law to drink, who then hands it to the bride to drink. This is the only time during the seven blessings that wine is consumed.

> *Blessed are You Hashem our G-d, King of the universe,*
>   *Who creates the fruit of the vine.*
> *Blessed are You Hashem our G-d, King of the universe,*
>   *Who created everything for His glory.*
> *Blessed are You Hashem our G-d, King of the universe,*
>   *Who forms mankind.*
> *Blessed are You Hashem our G-d, King of the universe, Who*
>   *formed man in His image—with the form of a spiritual*
>   *image he is structured—and He prepared for him out of that*
>   *an everlasting structure [marriage]. Blessed are You Hashem,*
>   *Who forms mankind.*
> *May the barren Jerusalem rejoice and be glad with the*
>   *ingathering of the Jews to her with joy. Blessed are You*
>   *Hashem, Who gladdens Zion with her children.*
> *Be happy, beloved friends [bride and groom], just as your*
>   *Creator gladdened you [Adam and Eve] in the Garden of*
>   *Eden at the beginning. Blessed are You Hashem,*
>   *Who gladdens groom and bride.*

*Blessed are You Hashem our G-d, King of the universe,
Who created joy and gladness, groom and bride, happiness,
merriment, glee, gaiety, love, affection, peace, and
friendship. Quickly, Hashem our G-d, let it be heard in the
cities of Judea and in the streets of Jerusalem, the sound of
grooms, the sound of brides, the sound of grooms rejoicing at
their chupah ceremonies and young men from the musical
feasts. Blessed are You, Hashem, Who gladdens the groom
with his bride.*

It is customary in the Jewish faith to wrap a glass in paper
to be placed on the floor for the groom to step on and shatter.
This symbolizes how precious life is and how easily it can be
destroyed, either physically or in spirit. In all of the joy, we
must remember sorrow, and we must work together to support one another during this time. Some argue, with humor
and wisdom, that it will be the last time the bridegroom can
put his foot down. From this time forward, he should be
ready to negotiate!

Other Traditions

Here are some miscellaneous traditions that you may have
heard about that have no specific origin known to them.

- ✦ It is unlucky for the groom to see the bride dressed in her
  full wedding attire before the wedding.
- ✦ It is unlucky for the bride to make her own wedding
  dress.

+ It is bad luck to wear a green wedding dress, because it implies that the bride has been "rolling in the grass" before her wedding.
+ Bad weather on the day of the wedding can be good or bad luck, depending on the tradition.
+ Making the first cut in the wedding cake together is good luck, and symbolizes a shared future together.
+ It is the best man's job to protect the groom from bad luck.
+ It is considered bad luck for a woman to marry a man whose last name begins with the same letter as her unmarried name.
+ The bridegroom should wear a flower that is also arranged in the bride's bouquet.
+ Sharing the same wine goblet during the ceremony symbolizes that the couple will share everything together from that point on.
+ Tying shoes to the back of the car symbolizes good fortune.

Something Old, Something New

Many people have heard the poem "something old, something new, something borrowed, something blue, and a silver sixpence in her shoe." "Something old" symbolizes that old friends will remain an important part of the new couple's life. This can be an amulet of some type that is given to the bride to hold on to during the ceremony, or an old garter that is passed on from generation to generation. "Something new" symbolizes a happy and prosperous future for the new couple. This can be anything from a new wedding gown to a new haircut. "Something borrowed" is an item loaned to the bride to wear or use during the ceremony, but must be returned to the original owner to ensure good luck.

"Something blue" is part of an ancient Israeli custom. The brides in Israel wore blue ribbons in their hair to proclaim fidelity. Today it is more customary that the blue would be found on the garter worn by the bride. The "silver sixpence in the shoe" was placed there to ensure financial prosperity for the new couple. Today, it is more common to place a penny or a nickel in the shoe, but a silver dime or quarter could still be found. Silver is a precious metal associated with the Goddess, and most appropriate for blessing a bride on her special day.

As you can see, many of these traditions offer fun ways to make your special day memorable. More importantly, they are a great way to incorporate traditions from each of your different faiths together so that you can both feel equally represented during your union. Many of the traditions are not specifically religious, and thus could be woven together without danger of mixing pantheons in the actual service. As you design your wedding, you may find ways to celebrate that are new to both of you, but strike you both as being beautiful and fitting. I suggest that both you and your partner come to a mutual agreement about which of these traditions you would like to incorporate into your wedding day so that when you meet with your chosen officiant, you can identify the specific rituals that have the most meaning to both of you. Your officiant will suggest the proper order in which to place them in your service, so that they flow smoothly.

Above all, remember that you have both the time and the responsibility to design your wedding to fit your beliefs, your sense of beauty, and your hopes for your life as a couple. Fitting deeply held family traditions into the mix adds an additional level of meaning to the day as long as the central purpose is remembered.

Your service should portray that union. It should not be designed in a way that solely brings comfort to others. If it does, you may come to regret that you did not have the ceremony of your dreams.

CHAPTER 5

CHALLENGES OF NON-PAGAN
FAMILY AND FRIENDS

ONE OF THE LARGEST CHALLENGES you will have to over-come when planning your Pagan handfasting or wedding may be your non-Pagan friends and family members. It is likely that you have family members on both sides who either don't know that you are Pagan or are potentially unhappy about your choice to follow a Pagan path. Paganism is not mainstream religion, at least not yet, so you will need to address these challenges when beginning to plan your special day.

It is very common today to find individuals question-ing the more traditional religions in which they were raised. I often hear stories from people who say that the religion of their parents' generation just doesn't make any sense to them. A man who was raised Protestant shared with me that when he asked for an explanation of the Trinity, he never got a straight answer. He said that no one could ever explain it for him. A woman who was raised Jewish asked me why the women in the Jewish faith are always treated like sec-ond-class citizens. And a woman who was raised a Catholic told me that she never felt comfortable in the church. It was made clear to her from a very young age that in the Catholic church she was there to be seen and not to be heard.

All of these people found that they were being asked to believe in something to which they felt no attachment. I truly believe that the biggest problem of many established religions and their institutions is that the deepest connection to "God" is meant to be experienced only by the clergy through sacred ritual. This can be highly unfulfilling for the lay person.

Discovering Paganism

Since founding the First Church of Wicca, I have seen more and more clearly that people are looking for a deeper spiritual connection with the Divine, without all of the religious dogma that traditional religious institutions impose upon their adherents. Neither do they want to be forced to believe solely in a male deity, because they recognize the duality of male and female energy in all things. They have come to realize that they are One with all of Nature.

People tell me stories about the moment they realized that they were Pagan. Some have said they realized it when they were sailing on the ocean. They felt a sense of melting into the scenery. Some have said they realized that they were Pagan when they saw the moon fill the sky with all of her glory. There is a huge connection that humans make when we acknowledge that we are One with the entire Universe.

Additionally, it is clear today that parents have less influence over the decisions and lifestyles of their adult children. There was a time when a parent could say to a child "Do as I do" and it was the child's responsibility to follow suit, but today that is not the case. Children are growing to be more independent and self-sufficient. They rely less on their parents for moral support, which affords each individual the opportunity to find his own way in life and institute a code of ethics and religious beliefs that work for him on an entirely individual basis.

Today's generation is not affected by the guilt trip that the churches of the past have put forth with the threat of eternal damnation. Despite this, parents and grandparents of these New Age seekers may believe that their children are refusing to be "saved." They may believe that their children and grandchildren are doomed to an afterlife of misery or destruction. The responsibility of knowing that you have worried and disappointed you parents is a huge weight to carry around. It might appear to be easier to avoid this confrontation altogether.

Pagan Misconceptions

Coupled with all of this anxiety are the huge misconceptions that people have about Wicca. Wiccans have been accused of everything from practicing in cults, worshiping the devil, and performing sacrificial rites, to participating in orgies. Quite truthfully, I do not know any parent who would want their child to be involved in any of these acts, myself included! Too often, Pagans contribute to these views with ill-considered or outright damaging activities, just as members of Christian, Muslim, or any other religious tradition may form misguided or self-satisfying cults that prove dangerous to the members, their families, or the world.

Responsibility as a Pagan

It is up to each and every Pagan to be a living and shining example of our faith. It is not enough to declare that we are Pagan because we have a natural connection to Mother Earth or because we have read a pile of books on the subject. We must live as if we have a very deep spiritual connection to the God and Goddess. We need to show society that we are conscientious in the choices that we make, in part because we understand the Law of Three-Fold, that our actions for good or ill will return to us multiplied by three! Let us show society (and our families) that we do not need punishment-driven regulation in our religion, since we do not try to escape the consequences of our actions. We anticipate and welcome consequences as we work to weave a better world for ourselves, our families, and all our brothers and sisters.

We are called to be today's model citizens. It is also up to all of us to pave the way for future Pagan generations. As Pagans marry and intermarry we will be raising new generations of children who will share our love for the earth, every man and every woman, and of course, the God and Goddess.

Wiccan Marriage

Marriage is a loving spiritual union between two souls. Many people see marriage as a government-mandated and controlled institution that provides a legal paper to legitimatize their spending the rest of their lives together, but they are missing the crucial meaning of what a spiritual union is. A spiritual union is love that is deeply shared by two people who have complete trust and faith in the Divine to guide their future together.

Wiccans find it extremely important that their union be recognized and witnessed by the God and Goddess. We want the God and Goddess to know that we have decided to join with our soul mate and thus become an expression of one united soul. Others may express this as joining to become "one flesh"—their two souls weaving together to become one couple, distinct in themselves but united. Such a marriage, and the ceremony that marks its beginning, can certainly become more of a challenge if there are friends or family members who do not know about your religious choice, particularly if you are trying to arrange this type of union without letting them know.

I suggest that if you have made the decision in your life to follow a Pagan path, and if you have made a decision for you and your partner to unite as one with the God and Goddess as your witnesses, then you should be unafraid to tell your non-Pagan family and friends about the choices that you have made in your life. Often we are so afraid of the reaction of our friends and families to news like this that we try to avoid the topic altogether. We justify our choice to not express our religious beliefs to our loved ones by saying that it would shatter their world if they knew. We should remember that we can shatter our own world when we refuse to live by our personal truths just to appease others. When we make the decision to "avoid" this conflict based on fear of the response, we actually agree to live according to someone else's reality and not our own. This means that we are continually letting someone else dictate how our lives should be, or at the very least, how our life should be perceived. We then *live* the conflict. We don't avoid it.

Author and motivational speaker Zig Ziglar once said, "FEAR is an acronym for False Evidence Appearing Real." In a situation like this, what we fear is that the relationships with our friends and family will be damaged because they will not understand. Would those relationships really suffer, though, or is it *you* who suffers? And aren't *you* involved in those relationships anyway? When we try to avoid these topics in our lives with our loved ones, we are actually making a decision between the importance of our personal truths and our apparent relationships with our family and friends. How can the two even be compared? It isn't fair to belittle your own self-worth and dignity because of a relationship with a friend or family member. If such a relationship goes bad after your world-stopping announcement of your personal truth, it couldn't possibly have been a nurturing relationship in the first place. Remember this, too: we are not alone in wanting friends and family members in our lives. They make the same decisions regarding us. They can love us for who we are and what we represent or not, but that is up to them. Your announcement of your personal truth is not asking for the relationship to end. We need to decide that it is more important to be who we are, and less important to be who someone else wants us to be.

There can be many reasons why we do not stand up to our friends and family about our beliefs. Sometimes we feel that we do not want to destroy a loving relationship, other times we feel that it is just easier to avoid it, and still other times we don't think it is that important. But it *is* important. It is who you are! Don't let someone else tell you who you are because it makes *their* life easier. Instead, tell them who you are because it makes *your* life easier!

Now you need to ask yourself a question, and really think about the answer. The question is, who are you really protecting by staying in the broom closet?

Are you doing it so the other person can enjoy a nice relationship, although a false one, or are you doing it because of your own fear of conflict? You may argue that you say nothing because of a desire for self-preservation. After all, Wiccans and other Pagans alike are discriminated against, and sometimes threatened with physical force. Please understand that I am not suggesting that you should put yourself in a deliberately harmful situation, but I would like to suggest that it may not be the relationships, or even the fear of being hurt, that stops you from speaking your personal truth, but your fear of conflict.

When you choose to stay in the broom closet because of fear of conflict you are behaving as if an important part of you is something to be ashamed of. On a metaphysical level, you are agreeing to the shame, and proclaiming it, strengthening the shame instead of your faith. Instead, decide that you are going to be proud of who you are. Proclaim your truth. Decide that being true to yourself is more important than keeping a lot of pleasant but shallow relationships. Allow the truth of who you are to be the new foundation for healthy relationships. Your truth is unavoidable and obvious. Make it unavoidable by saying it out loud. Make it obvious by making it one of the visible parts of your life.

Learn to trust and have faith in the God and Goddess no matter what happens. You are in the arms of the Gods and They love you, no matter what. They are all good and thus want to give you all good. They love you no matter what your personal truths are, and impose no expectation of who you "should" be. They are delighted with who you are, and with the person you can become. They certainly do not want you to be ashamed of who you are. What a gift that is! Think of the God and Goddess Who love you unconditionally, no matter what. Think of the God and Goddess Who can give you the strength to be convicted in your beliefs. The God and Goddess will be utterly willing to help you sort out your personal truths, and offer you the strength and confidence to live them. The God and Goddess give you all good with perfect love and perfect trust, unconditionally. It has been said that when the full impact of your relationship with the Gods really hits you, you will move up to a new level of self-worth.

I have suggested here that *you*, as a Pagan, must strive for honesty in yourself. I have no suggestion that will "make" your family or your partner's family accept your Paganism, or accept you as you are. You must accept and proclaim who you are. The rest is in the Hands of the God and Goddess.

We all dream of having the picture-perfect wedding, and of course this picture includes the attendance of all of our friends and family members. We want them to look on with faces full of joy and approval. There is nothing wrong with wanting this. Take the time to think about the advice in this chapter. Spend time in meditation with the God and Goddess. If you find that you have legitimate reasons for not wanting to tell your friends and family members about your religious choice, then consider having a civil ceremony for friends and family, and a private handfasting for you and your partner. This option will allow you to feel that your union is solidified in the eyes of the God and Goddess and that you and your partner share a spiritual bond, and it will also keep the peace in the family at the larger wedding. Once your handfasting is recognized by the God and Goddess, then the nondenominational wedding becomes a formality for family and friends, and of course, gives your union legal recognition. This is the day that you and your partner will unite. Your service should portray that union. It should not be designed in a way that solely brings comfort to others. If it does, you may come to regret that you did not have the ceremony of your dreams.

Ultimately, the challenges you face with non-Pagan family and friends are yours alone, you and your partner. The same is true of your marriage, your future together, and the ceremonies you choose to mark and cherish the day of your union. No one, not even I, can map your path to an open, vital faith and a beautiful wedding and marriage. You, as I do, must leave that in Divine Hands. They can help you and guide you, even when you are opposed by others, no matter how precious they are to you.

Spend time talking to different officiants, meeting with them face-to-face, so that you and your partner can be sure you are choosing the right person to help build the foundation of your new spiritual life together.

CHAPTER 6

FINDING THE RIGHT OFFICIANT

ANOTHER COMMON CHALLENGE for Pagans planning a handfasting or wedding is finding the right person to officiate the service. Trying to figure out all the details of your special day is difficult enough; being Pagan adds the additional challenge of deciding just who is the best person to officiate your ceremony.

You will find added complications if you are a mixed-faith couple. One or both of you may, for example, consider yourself Wiccan but continue to observe some aspects of your original faith. More commonly, one of you may be Pagan while the other is a member of a mainline faith. Outlined below are the specific issues you may face when finding just the right person or people to perform the ceremony you are planning, mixed faith or not.

First and foremost, decide whether or not you want your union to be a legally recognized marriage in your state or province. If you wish to be handfasted solely in the eyes of the God, Goddess, and each other, you do not need a legally ordained or state-recognized officiant. Instead, you want someone who is well learned in the customs and traditions of handfasting, and is willing to work with you to ensure that your day is as romantic and special as you envision it.

Often, a handfasting is bound by the words, "As long as we shall love one another." This is clearly a commitment of love between two people who want to share a loving union together. To what end? That is entirely up to the two of them. In this scenario, the handfasting ceremony is more of an engagement. This engagement would allow you, the couple, to live together and "try each other on for size," so to speak. Then, if and when you decide that you are ready to make your union permanent, you could opt to have a traditional wedding or another handfasting declaring, "Until physical death do us part." Let's take a look at these scenarios.

Pagan Wedding Officiant Options

If you want a handfasting ritual and are comfortable with a traditional Pagan handfasting that does not incorporate other traditions, then your union could be officiated by a high priestess or a high priest of a local coven—your own, if you are involved in one. Another place to find local ordained and nonordained Pagan clergy who could officiate your union is on the Witchvox Web site (*www.witchvox.com*). On the Web site, just type in your state and click on Local Clergy.

Pagan Clergy, Friends, or Family

You may be just as comfortable with a Pagan friend or family member officiating the ritual. You will then need to

decide if you want your ritual to include your coven brothers and sisters, or just your family and friends. Many times
I have officiated nonlegalized handfasting rituals with just
the couple, out in the depths of nature somewhere. I have
also performed legally recognized handfastings with just the
couple and any necessary witnesses. Regardless of who is
present, the God and Goddess will be there to smile upon
you as They witness your spiritual union.

Several of the 50 states in the United States have special
one-day designations that allow just about anyone who is in
good standing with the community to perform a legally recognized civil marriage. There is an application process that
one has to go through at the Secretary of State's office in
these obliging states. This requires time and planning, but
if you feel that you know the perfect person, and she is not
ordained by a church, this is an option. An example would
be if you are a member of a coven and your high priestess is
not formally ordained by the coven or a church. You perhaps
wouldn't think about having anyone else perform the service.
This one-day designation could also apply to a friend or family member who for one reason or another you think would
be the right officiant for you. Usually, these designations are
not allowed for the same person more than once in a year.

Justice of the Peace

Every state has registered justices of the peace. A justice of the peace is an appointed official who has authority
from a state court. They are literally "keepers of the peace"
and will serve in the capacity that a judge would for minor
disputes. They are often attorneys. A justice of the peace is

appointed into office by the town that he lives in, as long as he is a model citizen. A record of this appointment is kept on file at the Secretary of State's office. There are usually criteria that determine the number of justices of the peace in a given town and the lengths of their appointments.

A justice of the peace is also recognized as an officiant of civil marriages, and can perform a marriage in any city or town in the state in which he is appointed. A justice of the peace would be more inclined to perform a marriage ceremony without any religious undertones, but I have met a few who were willing to officiate a Pagan handfasting. It would be up to you, though, to do all the necessary research and have the whole ritual laid out for him, so that you could tell him exactly what you need him to do.

You may decide that you and your fiancé want to write your own ritual for your special day. That could be a wonderful experience to share between the two of you, and could be the foundation upon which your whole union is built. I caution you, however, to be sure that you have the entire ritual laid out and written so that the justice of the peace can perform the ritual exactly the way you want. I also suggest that you rehearse the entire ritual with the justice of the peace a few times before the actual day. Even if this costs you a bit more money, it would be worth it to be sure that things happen just the way you visualize them.

Nondenominational Minister

A nondenominational minister could be a wonderful choice for your union. Quite often, a nondenominational minister is well versed in different faiths, and recognizes the importance of a truly spiritual union. She may be more open-minded to other beliefs, and be a valuable asset in planning your wedding. Many will also perform same-sex marriages with the same enthusiasm as they would a heterosexual marriage, as long as it is legally recognized in the state that they hold their ordination. You will often hear a nondenominational minister declare that there are many equally valid paths to the Divine and the key is in recognizing that there is a Higher Power at work in this Universe. There are several places on the Internet where you could find a nondenominational minister in your area. Find one by searching "nondenominational minister" with the name of your city and state. Word of mouth is a great option, too. Ask around to see who has performed the marriages for other Pagan couples. You are bound to find the perfect person who will integrate your Pagan beliefs into your marriage ceremony, if you are patient and take the necessary time to do your research.

Unitarian Universalist Minister

You could ask the minister of your local Unitarian Universalist church if he would officiate your handfasting or wedding. Again, you would have to give him a full understanding of exactly what the ritual would entail and explain his role. Keep in mind, though, that because Unitarian Universalists come from so many religious beliefs, the minister might not feel comfortable performing that service for you. He might say no, but it can't hurt to ask.

The Unitarian Universalist Church is one that does not adhere to any specific religious creed or dogma. They are, instead, governed by their good deeds and the religious principles that can be found on their main Web site (*www.uua.org*). These principles explain that all people and their religious beliefs are welcome in the church as they join together in spiritual community and fellowship. It is common in a Unitarian Universalist church to find people who identify with Christianity, Judaism, Buddhism, Paganism, or any number of other religious beliefs, worshiping together in the meetinghouse, side by side. In fact, many of the Unitarian Universalist churches have CUUPS charters (Covenant of Unitarian Universalist Pagans). You can visit the main CUUPS Web site at *www.cuups.org* for more information. Additionally, if you are a solitary practitioner and have always been looking for a place to experience the Esbats and the Sabbats with like-minded people, you might want to see if there is a Unitarian Universalist church near you. Even though many Unitarian Universalist churches do have CUUPS charters, there are no high priestesses or high priests, nor are there degree initiations or dedication rituals. Everyone in the group takes turns planning and running the rituals.

Co-Officiated Options

You could have a co-officiated wedding ceremony led by two ministers of different faiths. When the wedding ceremony is co-officiated, it is only necessary for one of the officiants to sign the marriage certificate. This means that if you have a high priestess of a coven, but she is not ordained by her coven or a church, she could still co-officiate the ceremony as long as the other clergyperson is ordained and legally authorized to sign the marriage certificate in your state. A justice of the peace, a nondenominational minister, or a Unitarian Universalist minister might be a good choice for this type of ceremony. This way, you could have whomever you are comfortable with perform the handfasting ceremony and any other Pagan parts of the service, and then have the other officiant provide the civil aspects to recognize your union. This officiant can sign the marriage certificate for you.

Pagan-Jewish Wedding

A Pagan-Jewish wedding ceremony can bring challenges of its own. I grew up in a conservative Jewish family and I think it safe to say that most conservative rabbis would not co-officiate an interfaith Pagan marriage. It is equally fair to say that an Orthodox or Hasidic rabbi would definitely not co-officiate such a service. There is always the possibility, though, that a Reformed or Reconstructionist rabbi would be willing to co-officiate a Jewish-Pagan wedding. Reformed and Reconstructionist Judaism are much more flexible and willing to accept interfaith marriages of all kinds. On the other hand, if you cannot find a Reformed or Reconstructionist rabbi to co-officiate the ceremony, then you could have a nondenominational minister incorporate some of the Jewish traditions that are outlined in Chapter 4, along with some Jewish prayers (whether they are spoken in English or Hebrew), and co-officiate with the Pagan officiant.

Pagan-Christian Wedding

A Pagan-Christian wedding can prove to be more challenging and I have found that it is the most common type of

Pagan interfaith marriage. I have devoted additional time to discussing this combination in the hope that you will find it insightful and also see it as a step toward religious tolerance. I have several Christian colleagues whom I have asked: "Would you be willing to co-officiate a Pagan-Christian wedding ceremony?" The answer is always the same: "No."

Keep in mind two things. The first is that I personally live in a very conservative Christian community that does not seem to be very open-minded to any other faiths. Secondly, my Christian colleagues also have valid reasons for declining. Their concerns often resemble the Pagan practice of avoiding mixing pantheons. Many Pagans seem to think that all Christians are against us, and are willing to do anything to "save" us. In my travels I have not found this to be true at all. There are certainly Christians out there who do not understand our faith and do not want to take the time to try, but there are equally as many Pagans who shut out Christians. In order for Pagans and Christians to live together in tolerance and understanding, we need to take the time to learn from one another in a nonthreatening way. This means that we can't always be on the defensive, but instead we need to allow the God and Goddess to shine through us as a living example of love and understanding. I can guarantee that there are as many compassionate and tolerant Christians out there as there are Pagans. In fact, I might argue that there are more tolerant Christians out there than Pagans because of sheer numbers alone.

Please don't be quick to judge, but instead give each individual person a chance to show his or her own worth, and hope that you are given the same chance in return. Instead of finding reasons to hate, let's find reasons to love one another.

Interview with a Roman Catholic Deacon

I will share with you the conversations that I had with two Christian colleagues of mine. The first was with a Roman Catholic deacon. He is truly a wonderful man and very open-minded. If he is prejudiced, even in the slightest degree, no one would ever know it. He is extremely tolerant of all faiths, and the work that he has devoted himself to reflects that tolerance clearly. I have seen him offer his help to anyone in need, regardless of their religious affiliation. He and I often have conversations about Catholicism and Paganism, and he has proven to me with his words and actions that he embraces my spiritual beliefs, even though they are very different than his own. I have shown him the same acceptance. One day, I casually asked him if he would be willing to co-officiate a Pagan-Catholic wedding. He smiled a very warm and loving smile and said, "I would love to, but I can't. The Catholic Church wouldn't allow it. I could lose my credentials."

I was not at all surprised by his response, and neither was I hurt by it. I knew it would not affect our relationship in any way. I did spend quite a bit of time reflecting on that conversation. At first, I felt badly that he was in a situation where he had to follow a rule that, quite possibly, he didn't believe in. Then I thought mostly about the wonderful loving and compassionate things he accomplishes daily in his ministry.

I do not need to ask him if he would be willing to give all that up because of a single rule that he might be in disagreement with. He wouldn't. But he did not have to think over the question I presented to him because the answer was already spelled out for him.

Interview with a Christian Minister

This was not such an easy question, nor was the answer spelled out, for another colleague of mine. This particular colleague is a Christian minister, but not Catholic. He and I have a wonderful rapport with one another, and often spend time asking and answering questions about each other's faith. I have a deep admiration and respect for this man because he is an absolutely committed believer in his faith. I am quite sure that he has a difficult time grasping my Wiccan and metaphysical theology, but he always keeps the conversation going, and is very respectful of my ministry. I find him to be extremely tolerant, and a true friend.

When I asked him the question about co-officiating a Pagan-Christian wedding, he had a difficult time answering it. His difficulty did not come from any questions he had about his own personal truths, but instead from a desire not to offend me. Thus, he wanted to be sure that he thoroughly explained his viewpoint. He stood strong in his beliefs. He shared with me that he would not be comfortable, nor would he be acting in good conscience by co-officiating this type of marriage. He also said that he is not the voice for all Christians. He first explained that his decision had nothing to do with his church affiliation, because he is not affiliated with any specific denomination. The answer for him lies more in the fact that he believes that "the Christian faith is absolutely exclusive in its claim to be The Truth, not one of the many paths to God, but God's one path to humankind."

He has always had a clear understanding that my own personal belief, and the belief of most Pagans, is that there are several paths to the Divine, none better than the other— just different. He has always made it clear to me that he does not believe that. The question of co-officiating a wedding highlighted that belief for him again. Who am I to question his beliefs? I would not tolerate anyone asking me to change my belief because it didn't work for them.

My friend then quoted several beautiful Bible passages in order to clarify and solidify his point of view. He also said that if a Christian came to him asking the same question, he would suggest that they marry another Christian so that in their mutual faith, "God would infuse their values, priorities, and character." He believes it is much better if a husband and wife are on the same page spiritually, and drawing from the same Source. So when I questioned him on his specific use of the words *husband* and *wife*, here, too, his views were not the damning criticism that Pagans might expect: "Though being careful not to fully sanction same-sex marriage (or the Wiccan allowance of living together prior to the marriage commitment), on the level of what you might call 'civil law,' I really have little objection to some form of legal partnership like a civil union. If one purpose of marriage is companionship, I'd hate to think that gay persons would be compelled to spend their lives in remote loneliness outside of a lifelong committed relationship. I'm sure they may also be as good or better parents, in some cases, than many heterosexuals, since parenting is more a matter of love and commitment than gender." He also suggested that when he speaks about a marriage joined in mutual faith maybe his views would ring true for Pagans as well. I personally think that, in some other lifetime, this may have been true. Today, however, we have a Christian-dominated society. There are, so to speak, many Christians to choose from when finding a mate. In today's Pagan community, there are so few by comparison. It is far more important to have an accepting and supportive life partner, but less likely to find one of the same faith than it was in medieval times.

My colleague suggested that I could officiate the wedding myself, while incorporating some scriptures from the New Testament to show respect for the partner from the Christian tradition. I have actually done exactly that in several Pagan-Christian ceremonies. I am ordained in my state, and therefore I can sign the marriage certificate as well.

I will again suggest that, if your Pagan clergyperson is not able to sign the marriage certificate, you might want to ask a willing nondenominational minister to co-officiate so that they can incorporate the Christian side of your ceremony, and also make the marriage legally recognized.

Do Your Research

As for having a co-officiated interfaith marriage with these or any of the other world religions, I would strongly suggest that you and your partner do your own research to find an officiant. First, you might want to ask your partner if there is a religious leader from their local church that they would like to co-officiate the ceremony. Make some phone calls, or better yet, visit in person and ask the question, "Would you be willing to co-officiate a marriage with a Pagan partner?"

Be sure to exhaust all of your resources before determining that it can't be done. You never know—you might find that one clergy person who is willing to do it.

I would also highly recommend that you and your partner have some premarital counseling with the officiant of your choice, or even with a nondenominational pastoral counselor. In my own ministry, I do not agree to handfast or marry a couple if I do not have the opportunity to meet with them several times prior to the ceremony. It is important that the couple, whether they are both Pagan or of different faiths, have an opportunity to discuss with me, and each other, the challenges of being Pagan today. The couple needs to work together in love and compassion in order to solve these challenges.

Another topic that is necessary to discuss is whether or not the couple is planning on raising children, either from this union or a previous one. It is important to discuss whether or not the children will be exposed to the Pagan religion and to what degree, and what other faiths the children will be exposed to. The partners need to plan how all of this can be comfortably incorporated into their family unit.

I find, more often than not, that couples don't even think about any of these things prior to marriage. This was the case with one of my parishioners whom we will call "Jane."

Jane came to see me for a pastoral counseling appointment. She was raised Roman Catholic, but had become Pagan, practicing solitary Wicca for a long time. Just two weeks from the day that I met with her she was having her son christened. She was very sad, and expressed deep remorse for this, but she felt she had no choice. Jane is married to a man who knows that she is Pagan and is very supportive of her religious beliefs. He is a devout Roman Catholic, as are his parents. When they had their first child, there was no question that he would be christened in the Catholic Church. She felt terribly guilty about this, and did not know what to do about this situation; she asked me what I thought she should do. When I asked her what her biggest concern was, she said that she wanted her child raised Pagan (Wiccan, to be precise). I told Jane that I was surprised by her unhappiness. I told her that she would be giving her child a gift in a couple of weeks that most parents do not give their children. By allowing her son to be christened, all she is doing is giving him an option later in life. As he grows up, she may decide to expose him to the teachings of Wicca, too. For all she knows, he may decide when he gets older that he does not want to be Catholic or Pagan, but something altogether different. I told her that her gift of open-mindedness and acceptance is all that her child needs from her right now. She agreed.

My point in telling you this story is to emphasize the importance of you and your partner being on the same page spiritually, regardless of the number of sides to that page. If you love one another enough to marry without making religion a reason to walk away, then do the same for your children. Show them from a very young age that you are religiously tolerant of other faiths, so that when they decide what faith they want to be, they will know without any doubt that you will be there to support them. You begin this lifelong process by finding an officiant who can meet that challenge with you.

As you can see, there are several reasons to find the right officiant. Do not take this task lightly. Spend time talking to different officiants, meeting with them face-to-face. Bring a list of questions and ideas that you have about your special day. Ask the God and Goddess for guidance when making this decision, so that you and your partner can be sure you are choosing the right person to help build the foundation of your new spiritual life together.

In the eyes of the God and Goddess, your union is precious, regardless of where or when it occurs. Your service and the honeymoon that might follow may press your financial and personal means, but should never break them.

CHAPTER 7

WEDDING BUDGETS, DATES, AND LOCATIONS

WHEN YOU AND YOUR PARTNER decide that you are going to become handfasted or married, it is important that you pick the proper date and location, paying special attention to fit it all into your budget. Figure out exactly how much money you have or want to spend on your important day. You just might find that the only money you can realistically afford is for an officiant to perform the service. If you have an officiant who can do the service for you at no cost, you may want to spend your money on clothing alone. Before you start visualizing the wedding of your dreams that is going to cost thousands of dollars that you do not have, figure out exactly how much you can spend. Then plan your day according to your priorities and your budget.

Wonderful weddings have been created with little or no money. Be resourceful and think outside the box. I will give you an example. My own wedding was planned with only five hundred dollars to spend.

Breakdown of Budgeting

You may think that it would be impossible to have a "real" wedding with that kind of money. We did it, and it was incredible. I will admit that, at the time, we wondered how we could do it and invite the almost two hundred people we wanted to be a part of our special day. This was how we did it.

Date

First, we had to pick our day. This was easy for us. One cold winter's day we were cuddled by a warm fire in the fireplace, enjoying one another's company. We took out a calendar and literally, with our eyes closed, just dropped our intertwined fingers on it. We agreed that if it landed on a Friday, Saturday, or Sunday and the moon was anything but waning we would do it that date. We landed on a Friday, and the moon that day would not be waning. We had our date. We spent a few moments in meditation contemplating the date, and knew that it had been picked for us by the Gods.

Clothing

The next question on the list was my dress. How could I possibly get a wedding dress cheap? I had decided that, even though we were Pagan, I wanted a somewhat traditional American wedding that incorporated our Pagan beliefs into the ceremony. So yes, I wanted a wedding dress. My sister had been married just a couple of years before and I remember her wedding dress being only ankle length, simple but elegant. I asked her if she still had it and if I could wear it. She said that she did still have it and that she would be honored to have me wear it. I didn't even need to have it altered—it fit perfectly. My husband had two best men, and asked them to wear nice suits. My sister was my matron of honor, and she wore a very beautiful dress that she already owned.

Music

At the time of our wedding, my husband's twin brother was playing the trumpet in a really great jazz band. My husband asked him if he thought the band would be willing to play for us at our wedding. He told us that he would play for free, but the other three guys in the band wanted fifty dollars each to cover their expenses. We agreed. We had now spent one hundred and fifty dollars out of our five hundred dollar budget, leaving us with three hundred and fifty dollars.

Officiant

Next, we wondered who would marry us. We wanted our union to be legally recognized, but also wanted it to be recognized in the eyes of the God and Goddess. After interviewing several potential officiants, we agreed on a local justice of the peace. He was quite comfortable with performing the ritual and service just the way we wanted it. He only asked us for fifty dollars. Now we had spent three hundred from our five hundred dollar budget, leaving us with two hundred dollars.

Location

The biggest question we had was "Where are we going to have our wedding?" As Pagans, we really wanted to have it outdoors, but we were also concerned about all of the guests and the weather. We had picked a date during what is considered the rainy season here in Massachusetts, so we wanted to be sure that there was a backup location, just in case. My sister-in-law owns a golf course. We figured it would be the perfect place if we could convince her to let us use it at no cost. We could have the service out on the grass and then have the reception indoors, or in the case of rain have everything indoors, with the windows overlooking the golf course. My sister-in-law agreed, and was more than willing to let us use her space. We agreed on a cash bar so that she could generate a little income from the event, and we wouldn't have to worry about paying for everyone's drinks. Needless to say, it rained. Everything was indoors, but we had no worries because it was planned ahead of time.

Food

Now, the food was another story. We were inviting almost two hundred people, and had nothing to feed them. We thought about doing a potluck dinner, but wondered if there was something else that we could do instead. We spoke to my husband's mother about it, and she said that she would make the food, even if it was only finger sandwiches. That was exactly what we served, and everyone seemed to enjoy them. Another sister-in-law was kind enough to make us our wedding cake, too. All of this at no additional expense.

Pictures

We had heard of several friends who put disposable cameras on the tables to take pictures for the bride and groom, but we wanted some formal pictures of the families and wedding party together. I remembered that my uncle used to dabble in photography. He was never a professional, but he did great work and I knew he had a good camera. I asked him if he would take the pictures at the wedding. He is a wonderful guy, and he jumped at the idea, figuring it would give him a better chance to know my husband's family and our friends. My uncle did a terrific job, and took almost 300 pictures for us. We didn't stop there. We wanted our wedding videotaped, too. My sister had a video camera, but she was part of the wedding party. I asked her if we could borrow her video camera and have someone else do the filming. She suggested that her husband do it. He was happy to be involved. It worked out beautifully. We still watch the video every year. All we paid for was the tape for the video camera, film for the camera, and developing at a local drugstore. We figured that if there were any really nice pictures that we wanted enlarged, we would take the negatives to a nicer film developing store. Today, all you would need for still pictures is a digital camera with memory cards. You could borrow some if you can't afford to buy memory cards, because once you put the pictures on CDs you could return the memory cards. This expense cost us more than it would today.

We spent one hundred dollars from our five-hundred-dollar budget on pictures, leaving us with one hundred dollars. We decided to print and mail our own invitations. They were simple and elegant, and cost us fifty dollars, including stamps.

Wrap Up
We still had fifty dollars left over from our budget. We decided to rent a tuxedo for my husband. We were able to get

the tux at a discount, and it cost us the fifty dollars we had left. I'm glad we did. He looked wonderful in it! The entire wedding cost us five hundred dollars!

Our wedding night was absolutely amazing. We had no problems along the way, or on that night. We were so in love, and knew we were meant to spend our lives together. Incredibly enough, all of this planning happened in less than four months. He asked me to marry him on New Year's Eve and I agreed. We were married on April twenty-fourth. Fifteen years later people still talk about what an incredibly fun wedding we had. If I were to describe it, I would say it was nothing less than magickal! As you can see, a memorable wedding can be planned and implemented with very little money and still be enjoyed by all. All it takes is a little creativity and a strong desire to make it work.

Choosing the Date

The actual date of your wedding can be chosen as simply as the way my husband and I picked it, or with a great deal more thought and planning. No matter how you pick your day, if you are relaxed and in tune with the God and Goddess, and use your intuition, you will know when you have the right date. Here are some magickal influences that you may wish to take into consideration when you choose your date.

Waning Moon
Some would argue that a waning moon is the least desirable moon phase for embarking on a new life together. A

waning moon is a time to let go and release negativity in your life. It is not suggested that you start anything new on a waning moon, and I am quite sure that you will not feel as if you have something to release on your wedding day. On the other hand, a waning moon could be the perfect day for you to solidify your union. You will be releasing your immaturity, your childhood, your old life, and the life of a single adult.

Truthfully, there is much to be released in order to start a new life with your partner. You will then be able to move freely in a forward direction. Give it some serious thought and meditation before discarding a waning moon date. Don't discard it automatically.

Waxing Moon

A waxing moon is a wonderful moon phase to solidify your union. This is a time that is good for starting new projects. They will only continue to swell into something bigger and better as the moon continues to grow. When you and your partner unite, the plan is to have a long happy life together and grow in mutual love and respect. This is an ideal moon phase to start such an endeavor.

Full Moon

A full moon is also an excellent choice for your union. "When the moon rides at her peak, then the heart's desire seek," according to the Wiccan Rede. You are most certainly seeking your heart's desire when you unite on a full moon. You can rest assured that the Goddess will bring your loving union to a full manifestation.

New Moon

Again, some might argue that the new moon is not the best moon phase to unite because the Goddess is in Her resting state awaiting rebirth. She remains in this resting state so that She can regain Her strength and energy until She is ready to re-emerge into the night sky. I disagree that it is automatically a poor time to solidify your union. I think it could prove to be a wonderful time. Even though the Goddess is resting, there is nothing that would make Her happier than to see that two of Her children are joining in love and happiness during Her time off. This will only fill Her heart with joy and anticipation as She waits to return refreshed.

The new moon is a wonderful time to embark on new beginnings, and that is exactly what you are planning—to embark on a new beginning, together. Remember, while She is resting, She is closest in the sky to the blazing, life-giving force of Her Consort, the God. It is a time too private for us to see Her, but we know where She is. Remember also that, as a Loving Mother, she *always* has time to hear from us and be with us when we call Her.

Day of the Week

Once you have examined the moon phases, you will want to take a look at the day of the week. Is it a Friday, Saturday, or Sunday? There are also several separate considerations with astrological factors that can help you determine the best day, and even the time of day, but I would recommend that you seek the advice of a professional astrologer on that one. At the very least there are astrology reports that you can purchase online for this information.

Using a Pendulum to Determine the Date

If you wish to use a magickal tool to help you select the perfect date for your union, my suggestion would be to use a pendulum. This is a wonderfully intuitive way to pick it. I am sure that if my husband and I had had a pendulum at the time we had decided to marry, we would have chosen our day with it. (I am not convinced, though, that it would have been any more effective than intertwining our fingers and with our eyes closed just picking our date.) If you already have a pendulum that you want to use, fine. If not, then I would suggest getting a rose quartz one for love. The first thing you and your partner will want to do is pick the year. You can include this decision when following the directions below for picking your month and day, but most people know what year in which they want to handfast or marry. Today it is not unusual to be engaged for two or three years while one or both partners finish school, or until they can save up enough money to live on their own together.

Once you pick the year, buy a calendar that includes the months of that year, one month per page. If you find that the year is too far along to purchase a calendar, then go to the Internet to find one. If you cannot go online, you can figure out the dates and make your own. The general idea is that you want a piece of paper for every month of the year, with the title of the month at the top and each date in its proper location inside boxes. Once you have this done, put the calendar aside while you and your partner cleanse and charge your pendulum (see below). Be sure to do this exercise together. Choosing the date upon which to begin sharing your lives together is a very important decision, and you should both share in the entire process.

How to Use a Pendulum to Select the Date

If you have a home altar, use it. If you do not have a home altar, find a sacred space in your home or outside to do this work. You do not need to cast a circle when you cleanse and charge your pendulum.

Together with your partner at your altar or your sacred space, light some cleansing incense. If you do not have pre-made cleansing incense, you can use frankincense or a combination of frankincense and myrrh. Another good option for cleansing incense is cedar wood chips. Once the incense is lit, spend a moment letting the smoke fill the room.

Once the room is filled with the cleansing incense smoke, you will both need to hold the pendulum with your projecting hand. This is the hand that you write with. Hold your hands together while holding the pendulum over the incense. While your hands are intertwined, allow the smoke to envelop the crystal, the chain, and your hands. Think positive, loving thoughts about each other and your special day, being sure to sneak in some kisses. This loving energy will clear your crystal. When you both feel that the crystal is sufficiently cleansed, remove it from the smoke of the incense. If you have a Tibetan singing bowl, it would be a nice added touch to place the pendulum inside it. While one of you holds the bowl, the other can sing it. When you are through, place the pendulum on a windowsill that will receive the moonlight and the sunlight. Leave it there for twenty-four hours so that it will absorb both the female (moon) and male (sun) energies of the Universe. This should be done on a day when the moon will be in the sky actually casting light, as opposed to during a dark moon.

After twenty-four hours, retrieve your pendulum and gather your monthly calendar papers.

For the actual choosing of the date, you cast a circle. This will ensure that the date you pick is not influenced by negativity or outside energy. Make sure you have made decisions concerning the above conditions such as moon phase, day of the week, and astrological data beforehand.

YOU WILL NEED

A God candle (yellow or gold)
A Goddess candle (white or silver)
Candles for the four quarters (directions):
    A green candle (North)
    A blue candle (East)
    A red candle (South)
    A purple candle (West)
A small bowl of salt representing the earth (North)
Incense (love or psychic) representing air (East)
Another red or orange candle representing fire (South)
A small bowl of water representing water (West)
Your cleansed rose quartz pendulum
A chalice or glass with water, grape juice, or wine

SET UP YOUR ALTAR

Spend some time cleansing your space with the same incense you used to cleanse your pendulum the day before. Place your Goddess candle at the upper left-hand corner of your altar and the God candle at the upper right. Place the four quarter candles at the edges of your altar representing the North, South, East, and West. If you are unsure of where the directions are in relation to your altar, use a compass. Now place the representations of the elements (earth—a bowl of salt, air—incense, fire—a different candle, and water—a bowl of water) just inside the quarter candles. Light the incense and the candle representing fire.

CAST THE CIRCLE

Cast the circle in the following manner. Choose which one of you will begin. Pick up the bowl with the water in it. Place three pinches of salt into the water bowl. Stand and walk *deosil* (clockwise) around the perimeter of your circle, visualizing an intensely bright white light surrounding and protecting you and your loved one in your sacred space. Next, have your partner walk the perimeter of the circle (also *deosil*) with the incense, still visualizing the same intensely bright white light surrounding and protecting you and your loved one.

For the third time around the circle, hold hands and walk the perimeter of the circle traveling *deosil*.

Now say together, "Our circle is cast. Together we have created sacred space and will find the perfect date. As above, so below."

CALL THE QUARTERS

Call the quarters next. I suggest again that you both call the quarters together, to share with them the anticipation you have in picking your special day. Start at the North and call the quarters *deosil*. It is customary to face the quarter that you are calling, and bow to the Spirits when you welcome them.

North
"We call to the North, Spirits of Earth, be with us as the foundation of our learning when our special day will be."

Light the green candle and say, *"Be with us. Welcome."*

East
"We call to the East, Spirits of Air, be with us as the gentle whisper that tells us our special day."

Light the blue candle and say, *"Be with us. Welcome."*

South
"We call to the South, Spirits of Fire, be with us as the warmth in our hearts when we know the day is right."

Light the red candle and say, *"Be with us. Welcome."*

West
"We call to the West, Spirits of Water, be with us as the love we share with one another when picking our special day."

Light the purple candle and say, *"Be with us. Welcome."*

INVOKE THE GOD AND GODDESS

Next, you will invoke the God and Goddess. Choose who will invoke the God and who will invoke the Goddess. Don't automatically choose the man to invoke the God and the woman to invoke the Goddess if you are an intergender couple. Either of you can invoke either Deity, and you may feel called to cross genders in this particular circle. As you choose the day of your union, there may be something quite compelling in the woman calling to the God, and the man calling to the Goddess. Also, instead of just using the words God and Goddess, you may want to use the names of particular Deities, listed in Chapter 2. Be sure not to mix pantheons. When you invoke the God and Goddess, it is customary to face the altar and bow in respect when you welcome Them.

Invoke the God

"We call to the God, ruler of all that is sure and committed. Be with us as we choose the day of our union together."

Light the God candle and say, *"Be with us. Welcome."*

Invoke the Goddess

"We call to the Goddess, ruler of all that is loving and nurturing. Be with us as we choose the day of our union together."

Light the Goddess candle and say, *"Be with us. Welcome."*

PICK YOUR DATE

You are now ready to pick your day. Start by placing all of the months of the year you picked on the floor in a pile. (If you have not picked the year yet, then follow the same procedure and pick that first.) When you place the months on the floor they do not have to be in any particular order—it does not matter if August is on top and June is underneath it and so forth. Sit together in front of the altar facing each other, with the papers between you. Before you begin, you will need to tell your pendulum what you are looking for.

Tell the pendulum that you are trying to find the perfect date for your loving spiritual union. Mention all the conditions you have previously considered, such as moon phase, day of the week, astrological data, and so forth. Let the pendulum know that if it swings back and forth you will interpret that as a no, but if it swings in a circle you will interpret that as a yes. Then ask the pendulum to show you the difference to confirm the association.

If you have any specific months that you are already considering, go to them first. Hold the pendulum together in your receiving hands (the one you do not write with). Hold it over the name of the month, not a specific date. By using the process of elimination you should be able to remove all of the months that swing back and forth, leaving the months that circle. If you have more than one month over which the pendulum circled, you can start the process over again and pick the month over which the pendulum circles the strongest. You can place all of the months that you do not want aside and now just work with the remaining month.

You have probably decided not to be united on a day that falls during the week, unless you can find an officiant who will do it and the service is just for you and your partner. Few people would be free to attend a wedding on a weekday. So you can narrow your search down to just Saturday and Sunday, and possibly Friday. Using the same technique as above, with your receiving hands intertwined, hold the pendulum over the possible dates in the chosen month, one at a time. Pay attention to the reaction of the pendulum. Remember and affirm that back and forth movement means no and circular motion means yes.

You may find that the pendulum only moves in a circular direction over one date, but that date may have other negative magickal implications as defined by your choices regarding moon phase, etc. I would say that if the pendulum is telling you that one specific date is the correct one, all other concerns should pale in comparison. If you find that you have more than one date that received a circular motion, then consider all the other magickal implications.

If you are still left with more than one choice, use the pendulum again. Pay extra close attention to the intensity of the swinging. The day with the most intensity is definitely your day. Be sure to rely on your intuition in this ritual and not your intellect. After you have picked your date, spend some time together pondering it and discussing how you visualize it. Be sure to spend time in the circle hugging and kissing to reinforce the loving manifestation of your future date of union.

RELEASE THE CIRCLE

Now that you have found the perfect date for your union, you may thank the God and Goddess, release the quarters, and take down the circle. As you thank the Deities, you may extinguish the candle, or leave it lit until it goes out on its own. Be sure to face the altar when you release the God and Goddess and bow after you thank Them.

Release the Goddess

"Goddess, ruler of all that is loving and nurturing, we thank You for being with us when we chose the day of our union with Your gentle guidance. Stay if You will, leave if You must. Blessed be!"

Release the God

"God, ruler of all that is sure and committed, we thank You for being with us when we chose the day of our union with Your assuredness. Stay if You will, leave if You must. Blessed be!"

Now release the quarters. Start with the West because that is that last one you called. From there you want to release them *widdershins* (counterclockwise). Extinguish the candle of the associated quarter as you release it.

West

"Spirits of the West, of Water, thank you for being with us as the love we shared with one another as we picked our special day. Stay if you will, leave if you must. Blessed be!"

South

"Spirits of the South, of Fire, thank you for being with us as the warmth in our hearts as we picked our special day. Stay if you will, leave if you must. Blessed be!"

East

"Spirits of the East, of Air, thank you for whispering our special day in our ears. Stay if you will, leave if you must. Blessed be!"

North

"Spirits of the North, of Earth, thank you for teaching us when our special day is. Stay if you will, leave if you must. Blessed be!"

To releasing the circle itself, walk *widdershins* (counter-clockwise) together around the circle. Visualize that you are releasing the circle, that the bright white light dissipates around you as you go. When you have walked the perimeter of the circle, face the altar together and say, "This circle is released, but never broken. Merry meet, merry part, and merry meet again!"

The Pagan or Wiccan Wheel of the Year

Some Wiccans pick their wedding date according to the Witches' Wheel of the Year. Each Sabbat has a special energy that can enrich your handfasting in a different way.

Samhain

Samhain (pronounced "SAH-win") is the Pagan New Year and the beginning of winter, falling on October thirty-first. At this time, the God has died and is resting in contemplation and introspection of the past year. He is awaiting rebirth in the Goddess's womb. I have known several Pagan couples who have married on this date, and I think it could prove to be quite romantic. How better to ring in the New Year than with a celebration of a loving relationship? The best part is that it is the time of year when the veil between the physical and spiritual worlds is the thinnest. You can be assured that all of your ancestors will attend!

Yule

Yule (pronounced "YOOL") is celebrated on or around December twenty-first, and is the winter solstice (the longest night of the year in the Northern Hemisphere). It is the time of year when the God is reborn. From here on we will begin to see more daylight with each passing day. Yule marks the growing strength of the sun, similar to the waxing moon, and could prove to be a great time of year for a marriage. Depending on your geographic location, you may wish to keep distant relatives and the possibility of inclement weather in mind. One more thing to think about during this time of year is the religion of your wedding guests. If you have Christian or Jewish relatives, this may not be the best time of year for them to attend a wedding, since they may be busy observing their own family holidays.

Imbolc

Imbolc (pronounced "IM-bolk") is celebrated on February second. This is the time of year when we remember that spring is right around the corner. The days are growing longer and if we are lucky we can see new life beginning to spring from earth. The God is a small child at this time, and growing at a rapid rate. With Imbolc's association of new beginnings, this could be a wonderful time of year for a wedding.

Ostara

Ostara (pronounced "oh-STAH-rah") is the spring equinox, and falls on or around March twenty-first. Day and night are equal in length. At this point on the Wheel the

God and Goddess have reunited as a young new couple in love. They are beginning Their courtship and the earth is sprouting new life everywhere. I would once again caution you that if you have Christian and Jewish relatives, Easter is near this time, so this may not be the best time for them to attend a wedding.

Beltane

Beltane (pronounced "BELL-tain") is celebrated on May first. I mentioned earlier that in some traditions it is bad luck to marry in May, but with that being said, Beltane is symbolic of the marriage of the God and Goddess. They are clearly celebrating their union in handfasting or marriage and it is marked by the celebration of the Maypole. This could be such a fun time of year to marry, especially if you could get your guests to participate in a Maypole celebration.

Litha

Litha (pronounced "LEE-tha") is the summer solstice, or midsummer, and is celebrated on or around June twenty-first. This is the time during the Witches' Wheel of the Year when the God is at full strength, paralleling the phase of the moon when it is full. June has always been the most popular month to marry, and you may want to join the many who have wed in this month before you.

Lughnassad

Lughnassad (pronounced "lew-NAH-sah" or "LEW-nah-sah") is celebrated on August second. It is the first harvest, a time to reap the benefits of what you have sown. Certainly marriage could be reaping the benefit of a well-sown court-ship. This time of year can be extremely hot in some areas, another thing to consider when you are inviting guests.

Mabon

Mabon (pronounced "MAH-bonn") is the fall equinox, the time of the second harvest. It is celebrated on or around September twenty-first. This is the time of year where light and dark are in balance again. By this time, trees are starting to turn to their fall colors. There is nothing more beautiful than the trees when the leaves are turning fabulous shades of red, orange, and rust as they begin to slumber for the winter. By October, the early weeks of your new marriage will have an absolutely breathtaking backdrop, the perfect follow-through for your special day.

In all of this, I encourage you to listen to your intuition and let the God and Goddess guide you in choosing the perfect time of year, month, and day of your union.

Choosing the Location of Your Wedding

One of the most important factors in choosing the location of your wedding is whether or not you want to have it indoors or outdoors. You will also need to think about whether you want to be married locally or at some far-off destination. I have seen people get married on a little secluded island, at Disney World, at the Grand Canyon, in their backyard, on their local hiking trails, and in the Eiffel Tower. Be creative and romantic, but work with your budget. Don't overspend.

Once you have a few locations in mind, use the pendulum to make the final choice the same way that you did to pick your wedding date. It can be so much fun to work out the details together this way, and it will make a great story for children and grandchildren to hear.

Being Pagan, you will probably want to have the service outdoors if possible. Keep in mind, though, the time of year and the possibility of bad weather. You want to be sure that if you plan a beach wedding, for example, you rent some tents in case it rains. This could be very costly if you have a lot of guests. Your best bet would be to do something similar to what I did: have a place in mind where you could easily have the wedding indoors or outdoors, depending on the weather.

If you and your partner are getting married alone, with just the two of you and the officiant, then ask the officiant if it is okay if he or she gets wet in the rain. If everyone is willing to take the risk, go ahead. If it rains, well, that could be quite romantic, too. You are certain never to forget it!

Planning and Budgeting

If you can afford it, hire a wedding planner. They are a huge help, and can plan your wedding from top to bottom, soup to nuts. They will shape and mold your day the way that you want it, but they will do all of the legwork—right down to booking the honeymoon if you ask them to. Make sure your wedding planner is open to the idea of a traditional Pagan handfasting, and work closely with him in order to incorporate your traditions. This book would be a great resource to give him; simply highlight the sections that you want to incorporate into your handfasting.

If you do not have the budget for a wedding planner, then you can do this yourself. There are wonderful self-help wedding planning Web sites that will give you a step-by-step process for the things you need to do, in what order, and in whatever time frame you should do them. It's amazing what help you can get online today. Another option would be to buy a book, or ask a friend or relative who has been through it to help you. Just remember the entire time that you need to work with and stay within your budget. Plan the most important things first and the least important things last. That way, if you can't do the least important things, it really doesn't matter.

You should start with a piece of paper on which you list all of the things that are important to you. Have your budget amount at the top of the paper, and start researching. If you need a dress, for example, think of all the people and places where you could get a dress. Start making phone calls. Ask around. Trust your intuition, it will tell you when you have found a match. Treat everything on your list this way and you will be amazed at how quickly and smoothly things will come together for you.

Be sure that you and your partner divide the list and work together on this project. It can be overwhelming to do it alone, and you also want to be sure that you both want the same things. Neither one of you needs any surprises the day of the wedding.

Here is a sample list:

Budget: five thousand dollars

The following items are most important to me:

Legal officiant

Dress

Tuxedo

Catered food

Disc jockey

Wedding cake

*Function hall, with indoor and outdoor capacity for wedding
  and reception*

Seating for two hundred people

Flowers

Videographer

Photographer

Wait staff or caterer

Honeymoon

Not so important

Live band and host

Dessert table

Wedding cake servers

To fly somewhere for honeymoon

Expensive centerpieces

Wedding planner

Open bar

You get the idea. When you make your list, be sure that it
is realistic according to your budget. Remember that, in the
eyes of the God and Goddess, your handfasting or wedding
marks the thrill of beginning your life as a couple. Be joyful

and loving in your choice of dates, locations, food, and decorations, and plan the day with the same care that you would take in planning a major magickal work or spell.

In the eyes of the God and Goddess, your union is precious, regardless of where or when it occurs. Your service and the honeymoon that might follow may press your financial and personal means, but should never break them. Think of them as gifts to each other, to your guests, and to the God and Goddess. Your wedding should be a lift to your spirits, not a burden on your lives. You can then expect to see the joy in the eyes of the God and Goddess reflected in the joy and tears in your guests' faces, and in the faces of you and your loved one.

The list of possible themes is endless.
If you can think it up, and it has meaning
to you and your partner, it can be
incorporated into a wedding theme.

CHAPTER 8

CEREMONY THEMES

EVERY WEDDING SHOULD BE carefully planned and executed exactly the way the couple getting married wants it. The ceremony itself can be a wonderful opportunity for you to show the guests a little bit about who you are and what you enjoy. Planning a theme wedding is an opportunity for a couple to be creative and use their imaginations to ensure that their day is perfect for them. Here are some suggestions for themes, and how you can incorporate them into your special day. Remember, though, that nothing is set in stone. You can take these ideas, alter them, or make up your own. Your wedding day is solemn and sacred, but that doesn't mean it can't be filled with laughter, fantasy, and just plain fun.

Sabbat Themes

Although there are many traditional themes to choose from when planning your wedding, as a Pagan you might find it more meaningful to plan your wedding during one of the following Sabbats. I have included some ideas on how to incorporate the theme into your special day.

Samhain or Halloween Theme

A Gothic wedding theme could be perfect for a Pagan-only couple. The clothing style could be primarily black, somewhat medieval or punk looking, but definitely Witchy. There are many styles of gothic clothing in dresses, long skirts, short skirts, pants, long-sleeved shirts, short-sleeved shirts and more—the list is endless. It would be in keeping with the gothic style for a Wiccan to wear a cloak or cape over this type of clothing. When you walk into the room to exchange your vows, consider walking in together, to an almost completely dark room, carrying a silver candelabrum with lit black taper candles. Draw Halloween into the theme as well, decorating with cobwebs that house plastic spiders, and setting out carved pumpkin centerpieces filled with black tulips or roses. The favors could consist of small cauldrons filled with candy corn or a black votive candle. You might want plenty of bats hanging from the ceiling and decorated sugar cookies shaped like bats, cats, and witches. Also, be sure that the DJ has plenty of Halloween music on hand, including "The Monster Mash." If you went with a live band, you could ask them to join in the fun and dress according to your theme. The tables could be decorated with white or orange tablecloths and have smaller black ones on top. There should be plenty of black candles lit everywhere. You could really have a fun time with this one, and the decorations could be saved to decorate your home on Samhain as a yearly reminder of your special day together.

Mabon or Fall Equinox Theme

A fall theme can be one of the most beautiful that you could use. There is nothing like the smell of the clean crisp air in the fall and the beauty of the leaves changing color. If you spent a few days before the wedding collecting the colored leaves off the trees, these would make fabulous decorations. You would want your tables covered with white tablecloths, covered with smaller brown ones. The leaves that you collected could be scattered on the tables, and the centerpieces could be cornucopias filled with gourds. It would be really spectacular to have the bride's headpiece made out of the leaves, too, with the veil hanging from that. The food could consist of a traditional Thanksgiving dinner complete with pumpkin pie for dessert. All of the ingredients of a traditional Thanksgiving dinner are Native American, so your theme could include gratitude for the land and its lessons, including the teachings of the people of its first nations. Favors of leaf and Thanksgiving theme candles would be perfect.

Yule or Midwinter Theme

A Yule theme could be quite beautiful and would make any Christian guests attending comfortable, too. Decorations of pinecones, poinsettias, mistletoe, and evergreen garlands with red bows for accents all over the room would look so inviting. If you can decorate the day before the wedding, you might be able to bring in a Yule tree, strategically place red bows on its branches, and add a red tree skirt. Invite your guests to leave any gifts they have for you under the tree. The meal could be whatever your family traditionally serves at Yule or Christmas, but be sure to have hot chocolate and gingerbread cookies. The tables would have white table-cloths with smaller red ones on top, and the centerpiece could be a Nutcracker Prince and a Sugar Plum Fairy standing on a round mirror with holly around their feet, sprinkled with glitter or white snowflakes. The favors could include a Yule ornament with the bride and groom's names and wedding date engraved on it. If a lot of children are expected, you can even have a surprise visit from Santa. A friend of mine cautions, though, that Faeries love Yule and Christmas, with all the glitter, sparkle, gifts, and treats. Be sure to include dishes of sweetened milk at each table, or no one will be able to find their car keys when it's time to go home.

Ostara or Spring Theme

You could incorporate an Ostara or springtime theme. This wedding could take place in a floral garden, home to an abundance of fresh flowers, butterflies, and dragonflies. Pick a flower that symbolize springtime and new beginnings and place one in a small vase at each place setting. This will be your favor, too. The tables will be covered with white table-cloths with smaller tablecloths of pastel yellow, green, or purple on the tops. The centerpiece can be Ostara baskets, filled with decorated eggs or the plastic eggs that open with small candies inside each one. The centerpiece can be given away at the end of the night to the person who finds a flower, somewhere in the hall, with a tiny bumblebee attached.

If you have a lot of children in attendance, you can have an Ostara egg hunt planned for them. The little ones may keep the treasures they find.

Litha or Summer Solstice Theme

You could plan this wedding on the beach or in a yard that overlooks the beach. You could decorate with stylish citronella candles around the perimeter of your event, to keep the mosquitoes away, while at the same time setting the ambiance from the day into the evening with candlelight. You could do all of your decorations with seashells that you collect from the beach yourself in the weeks before the wedding. Use the seashells to make matching place settings, napkin holders, and favors that with a little imagination can be truly impressive. Maybe for your favors you would want to give each guest a beach towel imprinted with your and your partner's names and the wedding date.

Your meal could consist of a lobster bake or some type of shellfish dish with plenty of watermelon on the dessert table. New Englanders could plan a full-scale clambake with all the trimmings.

The summer solstice is traditionally a time for festivals and bonfires, and a time abounding with Faeries. It's also a time for first harvesting magickal herbs, so your party favors could include purchased or harvested bundles of sweet-smelling, medicinal, or romantic herbs. Even if you are not yet adept in the details of herbal magick, you can't go wrong with basil or other favorite aromatic herbs you can safely buy at the grocery store.

Be careful that you have the correct location, skills, and permits for any bonfire you might plan. You and your guests will want to remember the wedding and its magick, not visits from the police and fire departments.

Other Themes

Of course, Pagans are as much a part of modern life as anyone else, so your ideas for themes for the service, and especially the reception to follow, can draw from anything that you love, especially those things that the two of you love together. The two parts—the service itself and the reception after—may be quite different. You may not see some of the following ideas as suitable for your sacred union, but wonderful for the celebration that follows. On the other hand, it is *your* wedding or handfasting. Make it the way you want it!

New Year's Eve Theme

This wedding should be a formal black tie event. The groom should wear gloves and a top hat. Decorate everything in black and white and silver, with copious displays of the number of the upcoming year. The centerpiece should be a bucket filled with ice and a bottle of champagne in it to ring in the New Year. You could even go as far as to have everyone wear a mask that will not be taken off until the New Year rings in. The flowers should be primarily white roses with just a few red roses carefully displayed to balance the atmosphere. Your favors could be champagne bottles filled with candy, and the label should have a picture of you and your partner and the date.

Valentine's Day Theme

This theme is so appropriate for a newly united couple. You can decorate the room with red hearts and cupids on the walls, and pink and red streamers all over the place with red, pink, and white balloons. The tables could have white table-cloths on them with smaller pink ones on top. Have bowls of heart-shaped cinnamon candies in a crystal bowl for the centerpiece. Use your imagination, and include everything you can think of that is red, pink, hearts, and loving.

Other fun themes can reflect who you and your partner are, such as movie themes, fairy-tale themes, Goth or punk themes, decade music themes, or sports themes. Favors, decorations, music, and costume can all help make your special day truly a reflection of who you are.

The list of possible themes is endless. If you can think it up, and it has meaning to you and your partner, it can be incorporated into a wedding theme. The biggest problem you and your partner will have with choosing your wedding theme is that this will be the only time that you can pick one and there are so many to choose from. Pirates. Dragons. The wild, wild west. Be creative. Have fun.

You may choose to stick with the standard traditions with the bouquet toss, garter, and mountains of white flowers, or you may prefer a "standard" Wiccan theme with lots of robes, candles, and incense. Then again, your ceremony could be fairly conservative, and the reception as creative and offbeat as you want. Most of all, you want the entire day to be an expression of you and your partner, and an unforgettable one at that. So have fun, let your imagination run wild, and be safe. Above all, pick a theme that you and your partner will love to remember.

To wear a veil, or not to wear a veil:
that is the question!

CHAPTER 9

RITUAL CLOTHING AND JEWELRY

THIS CHAPTER EXAMINES clothing from a ritual standpoint, as opposed to the themed clothing information given in Chapter 2. Themed or not, you may want to incorporate some of the following ideas into your wedding or handfasting.

The Wedding Dress

Throughout history the wedding dress has been one of the most important features of the entire wedding ceremony. Wedding dresses are designed to ensure that the bride is absolutely breathtaking on her special day. The dress is a way to prevent any other women from standing out and "stealing the show." The bride is the center of attention on her day, and her spouse-to-be should notice no one but her.

In Britain, during medieval times, wealthy brides were adorned with expensive and lavish wedding gowns. They were made from the finest materials, and quite possibly cost more money than her family could realistically afford.

This was because in medieval times a princess, for example, would marry a prince from another country, and the family of the bride wanted to prove their worth and stature.

Many of the wedding gowns during this time period were made of costly materials such as velvet, satin, and silk. All of the fabrics were handmade and hand-dyed. Only the wealthy could afford such vivid colors as purple or red. In addition to expensive materials, the dresses would be adorned with precious stones sewn into the fabric to allow the bride to further shimmer and glow on her special day. Just as it is done today, when a lower class or poorer bride married in medieval times, she could not afford an expensive dress made of lavish materials but would have her dress designed to replicate an expensive dress as closely as she could.

The bride's dress was also part of her dowry, the wealth that she brought to the union in her own right. Her family would do its utmost to array her with all the wealth they could manage. Unless she married a ruthless man who might strip her of her personal wealth, she and her children would thus have a measure of safety and independence. A poorer bride might borrow or rent a beautiful gown, her only dowry being the memory of her bridal beauty resting in the heart of her beloved.

As discussed in Chapter 1, many superstitions were rooted in the wedding day. Because of these superstitions, traditions have been passed on from one generation to the next to prevent any evil forces from influencing the wedding day. The ancient weddings needed to have as much good luck as possible, as do today's.

The color of the wedding gown was one of the most important considerations in order to ward off bad luck and draw good fortune to the bride.

Wedding Colors

Tradition has shown us that various colors have been used to address a variety of superstitions. Below I will list colors and the magickal properties they would possess for your wedding day. This information can be applied to your gown as well as to your theme colors and decorations. I spent several hours in meditation with the God and Goddess to determine the most appropriate color to wear on one's wedding day, and below are my findings.

White or Off-White

White, or nearly white, has always been a favorite color for a wedding dress in Western culture, and symbolizes chastity and innocence. It comes from the creative life force itself and is actually the female aspect of this force. Additionally, it symbolizes the female mysteries and balances the bride's aura. This color is best worn on Sunday. It is common today to marry in a white gown even if the bride is not a virgin, but I would caution you against wearing white just because everyone else does, or because it is hard to find a suitable dress in an alternate color. Take a look at your budget, and if you can afford it, you might want to hire a seamstress to make your fairytale dress in a color that resonates with you personally.

Blue

Back in medieval times, blue was the preferred choice for a wedding dress. It was symbolic of fidelity and everlasting love, and was also strongly associated with the Virgin Mary. If you have Christian roots, you might want to consider having your dress made out of a very pale and soft blue. Blue calms and soothes, bringing peace to all situations. It is associated with female energy, and is best worn on Friday or Saturday.

Green

Green was an unpopular color for a wedding dress because it was associated with enchantment and the Faerie realm. In Britain, it was considered highly disrespectful to ask Faeries to participate during a time of transition and change. This would produce internal chaos for the Faeries, causing them to bring rain that could come down and ruin your special day.

On the other hand, you may feel drawn to using this color if you have built strong metaphysical relationships in the Faerie realm: you might find it rude *not* to invite and welcome the People of Peace to your celebration. If you do invite them, be sure to have plenty of sweetened milk in saucers. Avoid clanging iron. Add plenty of sparkly surprises hidden in your gown, your hair, and your flowers.

In ancient Rome, green was also a symbol that you had been rolling around in the grass with your lover before the marriage—a huge taboo for some folks, a refreshing breath of honesty for others. Green is associated with both male and female energy, and is best worn on Friday.

Black

In Victorian times black was considered the most undesirable color for a wedding gown. Most fabrics were very difficult and expensive to dye such a deep color, and it was considered the color of death, associated with funerals (as it still is today to the nonmagickal person). It was considered such bad luck in Victorian times that even the guests were not allowed to wear it. However, Witches understand the benefits of keeping negativity away by wearing black. For this reason black might be the perfect color for your wedding. When worn with white, black is associated with both male and female energy, and is best worn on Saturday.

If you and your wedding party are all (or mostly) Wiccan and family and friends all know you well enough not to be shocked, black may be the color of choice for your gown, as well as your robe, cape, and veil. Also, wearing black can highlight any other colors you add to the ceremony: flowers, ribbons, and so on.

Red

In China, red is considered the color of choice for a wedding dress because it is believed to be the strongest color for keeping away evil spirits. It is traditional to wear red with dragon and phoenix designs on the dress itself, because they symbolize the balance of male and female energy. In India it is also traditional to wear a red wedding dress for good luck. They do not wear a white wedding dress, because white is the color of mourning in these parts of the world. Red is associated with male energy and is best worn on Sunday.

Brown or Beige

Brown, or beige, is a rustic color and is clearly the symbol of earth energy. A great day to be married in brown or beige would be Friday or Saturday. This is the perfect color for you to wear if you need help staying grounded and focused, or if you already feel deeply grounded in the earth and nature, and want to celebrate this in your wedding.

Silver

Silver is the color of the moon, associated with female energy and the Goddess. It is a wonderful color to wear if you are looking to rely on your intuition. Your gown itself could be silvery satin, or you might achieve the same effect with plenty of silvery embroidery. Use real silver where you can do so wisely, but know that silvery substitutes can easily achieve the same metaphysical intent. Silver is best worn on Saturday.

Gold

Gold is the color for male sun energy and the God. It is associated with money and financial success, and most deeply associated with the true roots of such success: a warm and generous spirit coupled with profound optimism and hope. In the Nordic tradition, the tears of the Goddess Freya turned into gold nuggets as She searched for Her wandering (but faithful) husband, Odur. Gold is best worn on Sunday.

Gray

Gray is a wonderful color to wear for balance and harmony. It is the complete balance of male and female energy.

If you are having struggles with your extended families, this might be the perfect color for your wedding.

Gray is also associated with enchantment and boundaries between the worlds (spiritual and mundane, for example), as you can see at dawn and dusk, or during a strong mist. There is a saying that "at night, all cats are gray." You can see from that saying, and from your experience, that gray is not the absence of all color, but the balanced union of all colors. If your marriage is a center of an energetic and diverse extended family, especially regarding spiritual matters, gray may be just the ticket. Gray would be best worn on Sunday.

Pink

Pink is a great option for someone who might want to wear red, but finds it overbearing. Pink is associated with platonic emotional love. It is a wonderful color to wear for instilling caring and mental sharing without a preponderance of physical lust.

Nowadays, pink is also associated with various causes, such as breast cancer awareness and gay rights. These issues may be deeply important to you as a couple, or to your families, making pink the perfect color. It is a feminine color, and best worn on Friday.

Purple

Purple is the color to wear if you want to magnify the positive in your life. It is also the color associated with the spiritual realm, so it is sure to help you have a connection to the God and Goddess on your special day. Purple has often been associated with royalty, since historically it was extremely expensive and rare. Weddings have always conferred a measure of royalty on the happy couple (sometimes including crowns or tiaras), so this is perfectly appropriate for your special day. Purple is associated with masculine energy, and best worn on Friday.

The above are suggestions for possible colors for wedding gowns, tuxedoes, shirts, bow ties, or capes. Also, if you decide to have a unity candle ceremony as part of your wedding (described in Chapter 13), the colors that you choose for your wedding should also represent the outside candles used.

If you want to incorporate a physical handfasting in your union, you should be sure to pick two colors that have deep meaning to you and your partner for your handfasting ribbon or sash, and intertwine them with both silver and gold. This way you will be sure that you have the energy of the God and Goddess, along with your personal color energies, as the foundation for your loving spiritual union.

Ritual Jewelry

When we take a look back in history we learn that the ancient Romans popularized the use of engagement and wedding rings. The round ring is symbolic of eternal unity and endless love. Many Pagan couples choose to include an exchange of wedding rings in their ceremony. In the ceremonies that I have officiated, as well as all of the ones I have heard about, couples have done a ring ceremony. While it is true that a Pagan may not use a traditional wedding ring or a diamond engagement ring, some kind of rings are still exchanged.

There are several ring choices besides the traditional engagement ring and wedding band that you see most often today. Read the following suggestions for different types of precious and semiprecious stones that you could incorporate into your engagement ring, wedding band, necklace, bracelet, or anklet, given here with their magickal properties.

BIRTHSTONES

January's birthstone is the garnet. Garnet is associated with the first and second energy chakras. When affecting the second, or sacral, chakra, garnet will instill romantic energy and induce passion with sexual desire. When used with the first, or base, chakra, this crystal will absorb any negative imbalances found in the body, stabilize them, and direct new positive energy to the needed areas.

February's birthstone is the amethyst. Amethyst is associated with the sixth and seventh energy chakras. Commonly used in conjunction with the sixth, or brow, chakra, this crystal is best used as a tool for self-reflection and introspection, and will enable an easy connection to the God and Goddess. Used with the seventh, or crown, chakra, this crystal will help you relax and aid you in meditation. It has been known to gently open the pathway to psychic and mystical awareness.

March's birthstone is the aquamarine. Aquamarine is associated with the fifth, or throat, energy chakra, and will aid ailments in the throat. It has been known to soothe sore throats and swollen glands. It is a wonderful crystal for allergy sufferers, important especially if you think that allergies might affect you on your special day. It also calms and clarifies emotions by clearing the mind and allowing your inner voice to be heard.

April's birthstone is the diamond. Diamond is associated with the sixth and seventh energy chakras. Used with the seventh, or crown, chakra by way of the central nervous system, diamonds will help alleviate loneliness or depression. Used with the sixth, or brow, chakra, it will ease migraines and fear, and significantly reduce bad dreams. It is known to help establish your natural connection to the God and Goddess, providing the wearer with peace of mind.

May's birthstone is the emerald. Emerald is associated with the fourth, or heart, energy chakra. Emerald can balance emotional instability with peace and harmony. It will also help alleviate nervous tension and thus aid with circulation problems.

June's birthstone is the alexandrite. Alexandrite is associated with the seventh, or crown, chakra. This crystal will take lack of vision and depression and convert them into knowledge of the inner self, instilling spirituality and a sense of wholeness.

July's birthstone is the ruby. Ruby is associated with the first and fourth energy chakras. Used with the first, or base, chakra, it will help soothe feelings of greed and anger by infusing grounding and patience, and providing the necessary courage to change. In conjunction with the fourth, or heart, chakra, it will help the immune system by providing balance throughout your entire body.

August's birthstone is the peridot. Peridot is associated with the fourth, or heart, chakra. Used with this chakra, it will help lessen the feelings of bitterness and open our hearts to release anger to heal past wounds. Peridot is considered the crystal of forgiveness. It is also the crystal used to "heal the healer." This would be especially important if one of you relates to the other in a healing way, or if either of you works in a healing profession.

September's birthstone is the sapphire. Sapphire is associated with the fifth and sixth energy chakras. In the fifth, or throat, chakra, it will help those who lack will power by instilling wisdom and truth. In the sixth, or brow, chakra, it will aid in the healing of ear, nose, eye, and throat ailments.

October's birthstone is the opal. Opal is associated with the fifth, sixth, and seventh energy chakras. With the fifth, or heart, chakra, it will bring out love and peace by naturally putting you at ease. With the sixth, or brow, chakra, it will give you the vision to see your life's circumstances more clearly. In the seventh, or crown, chakra, it will ensure that you are open-minded to unlimited possibilities.

November's birthstone is the yellow topaz. Yellow topaz is associated with the third, or solar plexus, chakra, and will help eliminate all toxins from the body. It is the crystal most often used to settle a bad case of the nerves and to help aid in healing an addiction, since addictions are often related to intense or crippling anxiety.

December's birthstone is turquoise. Turquoise is associated with the fifth, or throat, chakra. This crystal will aid in communication, allowing you to speak with ease and bond spiritually with your partner.

OTHER CRYSTALS

Apache tear, or black obsidian, is a crystal that is black, but in the sunlight it can shimmer green. It is associated with the fourth, or heart, chakra, and when used with this chakra will aid in releasing all negativity caused by stressful situations.

Citrine is an orange crystal, associated with the third, or solar plexus, chakra. Used with this chakra, it will aid in instilling mental clarity by promoting self-esteem and focused increased energy while balancing and releasing unwanted negative energy. It is seen as a prosperity or "money" stone, but then, these are the natural results of healthy self-esteem and well-focused and strong energy. Find those first, and the rest will follow.

Hematite is a silvery-black crystal associated with the first, or base, chakra. Used with this chakra, this crystal will instill grounding and ease jittery nerves. By doing this, it will lower blood pressure.

Jade is a green crystal, associated with the fourth, or heart, chakra. Used with this chakra, jade will help keep peace amongst all people. Additionally, it will give the wearer the necessary compassion to deal with any situation that may arise. Compassion helps us solve conflicts with the power of love, instead of the love of power.

Malachite is a green banded crystal. It is associated with the fifth and sixth energy chakras. Used with the fifth, or heart, chakra it will help in aiding to release all negative emotions. Used with the sixth, or brow, chakra, it will aid in blocking spiritual or psychic attack. This can include the most insidious attacks—those that we launch against ourselves.

Moonstone is a white, shimmering crystal associated with the seventh, or crown, chakra. Used with this chakra, moonstone will help create a bond with the Goddess and female energy in order to aid in continued loving relationships.

Rose quartz is a pink crystal associated with the third and fourth energy chakras. Used with the third, or solar plexus, chakra, it will calm emotional stress due to unexpected change. Used with the fourth, or heart, chakra, it will transform negative emotions into loving ones.

Tourmaline comes in many colors, and its various colors are associated with different energy centers, but the result is always the same regardless. It will aid in promoting self-confidence while helping you stay calm and focused. Black tourmaline is especially useful in helping you feel grounded and stable.

The Wedding Veil

To wear a veil, or not to wear a veil: that is the question! This information is here so that you personally can determine how you feel about the religious aspects of wearing a veil. If you are not as concerned about this, and *do* or *do not* want to wear a veil for other personal reasons, that's fine, too.

One school of thought tells us that the use of a veil on a woman's head—whether it be sanctioned for day-to-day use such as in the Muslim faith, or solely for worship such as in the Jewish faith at the Wailing Wall in Jerusalem—is an idea that has been passed down from the Old Testament. In the New International Version of the Bible, we find the following quote in relation to the veil: "Now I want you to realize that the head of every man is Christ, and the head of the woman is man, and the head of Christ is God. Every man who prays or prophesies with his head covered dishonors his head. And every woman who prays or prophesies with her head uncovered dishonors her head—it is just as though her head were shaved. If a woman does not cover her head, she should have her hair cut off; and if it is a disgrace for a woman to have her hair cut or shaved off, she should cover her head. A man ought not to cover his head, since he is the image and glory of God; but the woman is the glory of man. For man did not come from woman, but woman from man; neither was man created for woman, but woman for man." (1 Corinthians 11:3–9)

If this is where the idea of wearing a veil came from, then it would probably not sit well with many Pagans. In the Pagan faith, we do not adhere to the idea of women being subservient to men, nor do we believe that woman came from man, or that a woman was put on this earth for man. We Pagans believe that man and woman are equal forces in love and procreation, and that all life comes from the womb of the woman. This being said, if you subscribe to the belief that the tradition of the veil comes strictly from biblical times, you may choose not to wear one.

However, an opposing school of thought suggests that the veil is a tradition handed down from pre-biblical Pagan times, that it is actually a Pagan tradition. When Isis, the Mother Goddess within the Egyptian pantheon, died, there was a statue of Her erected in Memphis, Egypt, complete with a black veil that covered Her from head to toe. Underneath the veil read the words: "I am all that has been, that is, that shall be, and none among mortals has yet dared to raise my veil." It is believed that underneath Her veil, She holds all of the woman's mysteries that unlock the history of the ancient past.

When we look at the veil from this perspective, we can easily see that it is a valuable part of Pagan practice, and is probably where the Witch's cloak originated. This veil symbolizes everything from teaching the lesson of having deep respect for all that is unknown all the way to symbolically representing an unveiling of sorts. You could even say that when the bridegroom (and no one else, of course) unveils a woman on her wedding day, it is symbolic of the act of undressing her, so he can view her beauty for the first time prior to the consummation of the marriage, in which the bride and her bridegroom practice the Great Rite. So you see, the wedding veil could be an incredibly beautiful Pagan way to experience you union. In the bridegroom's unveiling of the bride's face, and in their joining together for their first married kiss, all of the Rite is symbolically expressed in a way that is both beautiful and appropriate for all present to witness. They are no longer bride and bridegroom, but man and woman, God and Goddess, husband and wife.

*You are free to use traditional flowers,
magickal herbs, or a combination of
the two for a spectacular display
of fragrance, color, and magick.*

CHAPTER 10

FLOWERS AND HERBS

THE ORIGIN OF the bridal bouquet goes all the way back to the ancient belief that strong-smelling spices and herbs would prevent evil spirits from ruining things. Today we see everything from the bride carrying flowers down the aisle to a floral headpiece in her hair. Her bridesmaids often follow suit, and even the flower girls have a specific role to shower all of the guests with petals from the chosen variety of flower.

As Pagans, we are not limited to the colors, smells, and magickal uses of flowers. We can also incorporate the colors, smells, and magickal uses of herbs. You are free to use traditional flowers, magickal herbs, or a combination of the two for a spectacular display of fragrance, color, and magick. You can even mix and match flowers and herbs in the same bouquet if you wanted to.

There are several ways that you can incorporate flowers and herbs into your wedding plan. You can decide that you want to arrange the flowers and herbs that you pick from your own yard, or you can hire a florist. Either way, be sure to take into account color schemes from both an artistic and metaphysical standpoint, as well as any magickal messages or intent involved in the particular flower or herb. There is a list of flowers and their magickal messages in Appendix A for you to use in your planning.

Pairing Greens with Flowers and Herbs

Once you have picked the colors and flowers or herbs that you want to use, be sure to add plenty of greenery to pull it all together. Ivy (for the bride) and holly (for the bridegroom), woven together in garlands, along with other evergreens are especially valued for a wedding, regardless of the time of year. Ivy and holly (female and male) are magickally "paired," bringing good luck, protection, and fertility to both partners. Holly and, especially, ivy are "bower" plants: their foliage naturally creates bowers for airy protection and privacy, and thus are highly romantic. The "Christmassy" look that ivy and holly give a room should not be misunderstood. They were magickal, Pagan decorative foliage that were so well loved that British and German Christians just couldn't put them aside. Don't forget: they are evergreen all year 'round, and as easily available for a summer wedding as they are for Yuletide.

On a side note, all of these flowers and herbs have a connection to each other and a connection to you and your partner. All things in this universe are interconnected and come from one dual Source—the God and Goddess. If you take some time to think about this connection, you will be reminded of the beauty in all things. How you perceive this becomes your reality and your personal truth. Listen closely to your connection, your intuition, and feel the energy vibrations that you share with all things; become One. This vibration will help you make decisions in conjunction with the God and Goddess who reside in your own mind. You have access to all knowledge through this Universal Intelligence. All you have to do is listen and trust.

Real-Life Example

A perfect example of what I am describing here can be found in the approach of one of my parishioners whose daughter was getting married. When it came to his own daughter's wedding, he wanted to be extremely careful not to affect anyone's free will, but also wanted to be sure that there was at least one magickal display of herbs to ensure her protection and happiness in her union. He went to great lengths to ensure that this undertaking was successful, gathering the herbs from the homes and towns the two families lived in and thanking the land with gifts of water and fertilizer. He chose these twelve herbs, six associated with male energy and six with female energy, and arranged them in a vase decorated by his youngest daughter, the bride's sister:

Holly (male) from the bridegroom's home, for protection and good luck, especially for men.

Ivy (female) traditionally magickally paired with holly, for protection, good luck, and fidelity for men and women, and as a guard against negativity.

*Oak (male) white oak for protection, potency for males, and
    fertility.*
*Horsetail (female) fertility in all of its forms, but mainly for
    conceiving babies.*
Sage (male) for wisdom, immortality, and protection.
Violet (female) for love and harmony.
St. John's Wort (male) for health, protection, love, and strength.
*Mugwort (female) for strength, protection, healing, endurance
    on journeys, lust, and fertility.*
Basil (male) for love, wealth, protection, and exorcism.
Quince (female) for protection, love, and happiness.
Toadflax (male) for protection and hex-breaking.
Yarrow (female) for courage and love, and for healing wounds.

This man placed the arrangement on a small table to the
side of the couple as they exchanged their vows, then moved
it to the bridal table at the reception and dinner. He found
that the negativity he sensed from one individual he feared
would upset the ceremony dissipated. Afterward, he said that
despite the protective and supportive magick of the flowers
and herbs he had arranged for the ceremony, "the real bouquet at the wedding had only two blossoms: my daughter
and her young husband. They brought the real magick."

Meditation to Aid Selection of Flowers

When I think about the connection between humankind
and the gifts of the natural world, and the idea of being surrounded with flowers and herbs and all of their beautiful

and magickal attributes, I am inspired. I have included the following guided meditation to help put you and your fiancé in the proper frame of mind to make decisions about your flowers and herbs for your ceremony. It would be helpful if you or your fiancé could record this meditation before undertaking it, speaking slowly and deliberately into the recorder. Then, when you are ready to start your meditation together you can find a spot that is quiet and serene, while you play soft meditation music in the background, or the sounds of a lake, a stream, or birds. Read all of the following into your tape recorder, then play it back when you undertake the meditation.

Meditation

"Get yourselves into a comfortable meditative position, holding hands or resting next to each other. Close your eyes and take three deep breaths, in through your nose and out through your mouth. Feel your body and muscles relax with each breath that you take. Notice the rhythm of your breath and become one with your breathing pattern. Now let's begin."

"It is a warm spring day. The sun is shining so brightly that it could easily be summer if it were a later month, but it is spring. You are in an open field, but as you look around you notice that the edges of this field are bordered with an amazing display of vibrant, fragrant flowers. You and your fiancé are alone together. As you approach the border of flowers, you notice a short white picket fence behind the natural floral border. There are several flowers and herbs from behind the picket fence peeking through the stakes. You realize that this fence goes on forever, intended to keep you away from the natural beauty that hides behind the fence. You both decide that there must be a gate that will allow you access. Traveling *deosil* (clockwise), you follow the fence, noticing all of the different colors and aromas of the flowers and herbs along the border. Take a few moments in silence together to see how clearly the physical world you are standing in, and the unknown realm on the other side of the fence, are separating you. Use your intuition to guide you to the gate that will ease your curiosity, and let you in." (Record ten minutes of silence.)

"Good work. You have found the entrance. You look at each other with anticipation and excitement knowing that you are about to see the other side, another realm. Approach the gate slowly and with caution. Together, carefully unlock the hinge and open the gate. The bright sunlight and spectacular, copious display of nature and wildlife are too much for your eyes. You turn away, your eyes in pain. Give your eyes a moment to adjust and then look again. There are flowers and herbs everywhere, and you begin to feel lightheaded from all of the fragrances. This does not stop you from moving forward. You slowly walk through the gate and see a dirt path in front of you. You both look at each other as if to question where it will lead you. On the edges of the path you are invited to view tens of thousands of different flowers and herbs, but you know that you should not pick them. Hold your hands out and ask the God and Goddess for guidance in finding the perfect ones, the ones that hold your magickal messages. Be sure to make a mental note of the ones that you are led to, because you know that you cannot bring them back with you.

"As you continue to walk along the path, you notice that you are actually surrounded by trees. These trees are protecting the flowers and herbs by allowing just the right amount of sunlight in, to foster their continued growth. As you continue your journey on this dirt path you notice an abundance of wildlife. You see the beautiful, multicolored butterflies and dragonflies with delicate wings and curious eyes. (Record three minutes of silence) Then your attention is drawn to the deer, raccoons, fox, and other wildlife. (Record three minutes of silence) And yet again your attention is drawn to the limbs of the trees where owls and parrots reside. Suddenly overhead, you watch a plethora of birds fly overhead—countless different species! (Record three minutes of silence)You continue to follow the path, now anxious to see what lies at the end, but you walk slowly and cautiously, being careful not to disturb this incredible place.

"Ahead, it looks as though there is more sunlight and you can hear running water. As you approach the end of the path, you can smell clear, soothing water and the sound is becoming less distant. Finally, you have reached the end of the path. The trees end here as well. Ahead of you is a beautiful but small meadow bordering a stream full of rocks, carefully placed by Mother Nature. You can see the water swirl and dance, intertwining with the rocks. Next to the stream, you see a large towel lying in the sunlight. You and your fiancé decide that you will lie on this towel together and take in all of the sights, sounds, and fragrances in this safe haven that you have been given to enjoy. There is no one else—just you and Mother Nature.

"You both decide that you want to become one with nature and disrobe one another, slowly and deliberately, taking in the sight you are unveiling. You have been given the gift of *seeing* each other, and quite possibly for the first time, but this is not the time to consummate your union. Instead, you realize that you have something much greater to look forward to with one another. You both enter the stream and play like children, trying to catch the fish and moving rocks around to change the direction of the water's natural flow. You splash one another and hug and kiss, but that is all. You continually look around at the natural beauty that is all around you, and your breath leaves you momentarily. You have become One with nature. You have become One with the water in the stream, the animals, the birds, the insects, the trees, the flowers, the herbs, and the God and Goddess. Savor this Oneness for a few minutes and recognize that it will not last forever." (Record ten minutes of silence.)

"Now you must return. You both know that you can come back to this place of serenity anytime, but for now you must return home. You step out of the water and dry each other off lovingly with the towel. You both put your clothes back on, and return to the dirt path, but not before you look at your surroundings once more. On your way back down the dirt road, you make another mental note of all the flowers and herbs that stand out for you, but you still do not pick any. These flowers and herbs are for your senses only, not for keeping. Walk slowly back and savor the splendor and beauty you are sharing with one another. When you return to the gate be sure to thank the God and Goddess for your adventure. You could say, 'God and Goddess, we leave the place we have come from undisturbed, as if we had never been here. We thank You for the honor of Your presence. For this we give thanks. . . . And so it is! Blessed be!' Walk through and close the gate behind you.

"When you are ready, open your eyes and come back to this place and time. Be sure to spend a few moments with your hands on the ground in order to let any extra energy flow from you into the ground to neutralize."

Now you are ready to choose your flowers for your special day! If you remember, as my friend did, that you and your new spouse are the most precious flowers of the day, and the hands of the God and Goddess the most exquisite vessels to hold the two of you, your choices should flow with surprising and magickal ease. Of course, you can add the advice of a florist, herbalist, or wedding planner. Pore over magazines, flower shops, and your own garden, along with those of your friends, to weave together a mix of herbs and flowers that says everything you want it to say, and sets your celebration in a bower you will never forget.

*Whether you choose to purchase your
incense and oils, or to grow, harvest, and
make your own, be sure to consecrate it
for its magickal purpose before using it in
any ritual or spell.*

CHAPTER 11

INCORPORATING INCENSE, OILS, AND SPELLS

THERE ARE MANY DIFFERENT WAYS that you can incorporate incense and essential oils into your special day, using their magickal or healing properties. Incense and essential oils can be used for ritual baths, burning, and spell work. Listed below are some herbal recipes, with ideas and spells that you might want to use, either as they are or changed to suit your personal needs and goals.

Incense

Incense is made from dried herbs, woods, and flowers. Many people grow their own raw materials and harvest them, because they believe that the magickal energy is intensified significantly when you tend to them yourself, feeding them with your own magickal energy. So certainly you can grow your own, harvest them at the proper time of year, and then dry them out for use as incense. As well, you can purchase incense that is equally as effective from an occult shop or an

163

herbal supplier, including those on the Internet. Those that you buy from others may be somewhat less personalized, but they can be magickally significant in other ways. They may come from a spiritually important part of the world, such as the Himalayas or the American West. They may use tropical or other types of plants or materials that you could not grow properly or find in your area. They may be offered by a particular group or business that you feel called to support. Finally, the particular product may be beyond your level of skill to produce, or you may need amounts for your wedding that are beyond your capacity to make yourself.

Essential Oils

Essential oils are made from several different parts of the plant, such as the flowers, leaves, wood, roots, seeds, or peels, depending on where the oil is the easiest to extract in the greatest concentration. They are also usually mixed with different carrier oils in order to dilute them, making them safer to use and to reduce allergies or skin irritation.

Whether you choose to purchase your incense and oils, or to grow, harvest, and make your own, be sure to consecrate it for its magickal purpose before using it in any ritual or spell. If you, for example, decided that you wanted to purchase loose rose petal incense, think about all of the hands and energy fields that this herb will have passed through before reaching yours. Let's say that you wanted to use rose petals in your love spell. Those roses would have to be grown somewhere—who knows where? They would be watered, fed, nurtured, and quite possibly touched and smelled on a regular basis while in the nursery. When they are ready, someone will have to harvest them, by hand or machine. Who knows how many hands they will pass through before they are properly dried and ground into a fresh herb? From that point, the powder will be put into storage containers and shipped by plane or truck to its storehouse destination. Then it will be reshipped to the occult supplier that orders it, to sit on their shelf.

Again, who knows how long it will sit on that shelf and how many people will feel compelled to pick up the storage container, open it, and smell and feel the contents inside until you finally decide to purchase it? You will hand it to the store owner, who will measure out the ingredients and place it in a new storage container before finally handing it to you. This doesn't even take into consideration the additional number of steps and hands it would go through if you were not purchasing it loose, but instead in the prepackaged incense sticks or cones.

Well, I wouldn't imagine that, after going through all of that, the herb you have chosen would not have at the very least been placed in the hands and energy field of one negative person. Think about everything you bring into your own life, and the days when your energy field would have been negative enough to affect those rose petals. Now multiply that by the number of people who handled the product you are buying. You can certainly understand the need to ensure that it is cleared of negativity.

Remove Negativity

The process of removing negativity from an object is an exorcism of sorts, but it is a bit more comfortable for most just to call it a cleansing and consecration. This act of cleansing and consecrating your consumable magickal supplies should not be taken lightly, nor should it be avoided. The energy field that envelops your supplies will affect you and your surrounding area, whether it is negative or positive. Practicing magick without consecrating your magickal supplies can cause serious problems. Remember, too, that when you cleanse and consecrate your consumable magickal supplies, you are working in conjunction with the God and Goddess. You are making the magickal purpose for your materials known to Them. They can now assist you in accomplishing exactly what you need to do with your particular magickal supply.

Consecrating Herbs and Oils

Now we know that we will be consecrating our herbs and oils for use in spells for our special day, but how do we do it? We start by bringing that item to our altar or sacred space. You do not have to cast a circle when consecrating your supplies, but some Witches prefer to do so. The way I look at it is that when I am performing a ritual, I will not use the representations of the elements I have chosen for my ritual without consecrating them first, so I do that before the circle is cast, not after. It would stand to reason that you could just as effectively consecrate any consumable supply in the same way.

A consecration rite is very simple, but, again, should not be taken lightly. You will want to spend a moment or two grounding and centering yourself in order to establish your connection to the God and Goddess. You will hold up your consumable supply and say: "God and Goddess, I now purify this incense (or oil) so that it may be released of all negativity, that which I can see and that which I cannot, and I let it be known that it will be used for [state its purpose]. For this I give thanks. And so it is! Blessed be!" As you speak the final words, draw a pentacle with your index finger or wand over the object.

Keep in mind, too, that if you do not use all of the incense or oil and you want to use it another time for another purpose, all you have to do is consecrate it again, stating the new purpose. This would not be a matter of cleansing (you've already done that), but of clearing the item of your original intent, and letting the God and Goddess bless your new intent for that item or substance. Now you are ready to use your incense and oils again.

Potential Ingredients for Love Scents

In Appendix B there is a list of potential ingredients for love incense, essential oils, sachets, and ritual baths suitable for your wedding or handfasting. The properties of those herbs are love, lust, friendship, attraction, fertility, and protection. I purposely did not list the exact properties of each herb, so that you can research and experiment on your own. Scott Cunningham's *Encyclopedia of Magical Herbs* is a wonderful book that will tell you the exact properties of the following herbs, but I would suggest that instead of relying solely on the books, take a trip to your local metaphysical store. Smell the herbs, and feel the magickal energy and properties in them. Really lose yourself in them, and your intuition will guide you to the proper ones to choose.

Your research and experience, including your personal attraction to a particular herb, may increase the list in the Appendix. You will probably find some on the list that are clearly *not* for you. In all of this, keep your intuition lively and mind open, and trust that the God and Goddess will guide you through the process, if you let Them.

Incense Recipes

All of the following recipes are for loose incense, and will need to be burned on a charcoal tablet. You can buy charcoal in an occult supply store. Be sure to light the charcoal with a match and place it on a heatproof surface. Once it has finished sparking and smoking, it will glow red. Then you can place pinches of your incense on it, and refresh it with new incense as you need it. The following recipes are included to provide you with a few examples of mixed herbs that can be used for a specific purpose. Read the name of the recipe and spend some time in meditation with the God and Goddess to determine whether you can use this mixture in a way that makes sense for your current purpose.

✳

LOVE IS IN THE AIR
Four tablespoons copal
Three tablespoons rose petals
Two tablespoons lemon verbena
One tablespoon catnip
One tablespoon mistletoe
One tablespoon lavender

NEW BEGINNINGS
Two tablespoons frankincense
Two tablespoons raspberry
One tablespoon peppermint
Three drops orange oil

THE MIGHTY APHRODITE
Three tablespoons patchouli
Two tablespoons hibiscus
Two tablespoons red sandalwood
One tablespoon orris powder
One tablespoon damiana
One pinch cinnamon
One pinch saffron

HEALTHY HOME
Three tablespoons myrrh
Three tablespoons green tea leaves
Two tablespoons benzoin
One tablespoon basil
One tablespoon orange peel
One-half tablespoon clove

FANTASTIC FANTASY
Two tablespoons Dragon's blood
Two tablespoons catnip
Two tablespoons benzoin
One tablespoon orris powder

THE HAPPY COUPLE
Two tablespoons frankincense
Two tablespoons thyme
Two tablespoons raspberry
Two tablespoons rose petals
One tablespoon catnip
One tablespoon lavender
One tablespoon lemon

✳

FOREVER YOURS
Three tablespoons myrrh
Three tablespoons frankincense
Two tablespoons rose petals
One tablespoon lavender
One tablespoon amber resin
One tablespoon Balm of Gilead

✳

ROMANCE IN THE AIR
Three tablespoons myrrh
Two tablespoons hibiscus
Two tablespoons jasmine
One tablespoon willow bark

✳

ESSENTIALLY SENSUAL
Two tablespoons copal
Two tablespoons patchouli
Two tablespoons passion flower
One pinch cinnamon

✳

MORAL VIRTUE
Three tablespoons frankincense
Two tablespoons red clover
One tablespoon orris powder
One tablespoon clove

PERFECT LOVE
Four tablespoons frankincense
Three tablespoons rose petals
Two tablespoons red sandalwood
Three drops magnolia oil

PERFECT TRUST
Three tablespoons red sandalwood
Two tablespoons lavender
One tablespoon lemon peel

AND IT HARM NONE
Three tablespoons myrrh
Three tablespoons red sandalwood
One tablespoon oak
One tablespoon hyssop

Spells

Herbs, oils, and incense have powerful magick whenever you use, handle, or make them, but you may want to boost or focus that energy by performing an actual spell using the materials. Wiccans use spells as a way to manifest thoughts into action on this physical plane. Spells can be a wonderful way to manifest the union of your dreams. Remember that it is highly unethical to perform magick involving others without their knowledge and consent. Truthfully, this applies to *you*, as well. Don't perform these or any other spells unless you are mindful and certain about your intent in performing the magick, and have prepared yourself, your materials, and the space you will use for your spiritual purpose.

—Oil Ritual Bath—

This would be a wonderful spell to do several times before the actual handfasting or wedding date, and then again right before getting ready for the ceremony. Remember that this is not a bath for cleaning yourself. Do that first. This is a bath for spiritually cleansing yourself. Also, be sure to use a basket or filter over the drain so as not to clog the pipe with saturated herbs when the bath is finished.

YOU WILL NEED
Two essential oils of your choice, one for relaxation and one for love
One dried herb or loose incense of your choice for meditation
Two unscented tea lights
Meditation music (optional)

WHAT TO DO
Light the tea lights and place them at opposite ends of the bathroom. Be sure to shut the main light off. Softly play the meditation music if you would like to use it. Run warm water into the tub to a desired depth. When the tub is finished running, take one of the essential oils that you have picked and add three drops, one at a time. After each drop say the following: "I soon will become one flesh with the love of my life."

Now you will take the dried herb or incense that you chose, and place a thin layer on the surface of the water. Say the following: "I am about to embark in a new *physical* world. When I splash through the surface, I will be joined as one in a new *spiritual* realm."

Slowly enter the water, and visualize entering the spiritual realm as you break through the layer of surface herbs.

When you are comfortable in the water, take the second essential oil and drop three drops into the water, one at a time, reciting the following after each one: "God and Goddess, You have given me an incredible gift in my loved one. I will honor and cherish that gift always. For this I give thanks. . . . And so it is! Blessed be!"

Enjoy your cleansing bath in a meditative state. When you are through bathing, drain the water and say: "My old life ends as I embark on a new journey." When the water has finished draining, collect the leftover herbs. Leave them outdoors in a special place, as an offering to the Gods.

————New Apartment or House Smudging————

Smudging is the use of incense or herbal smoke in an active, intense way to cleanse and bless a space or an item (nothing is marked with soot). If you and your partner have already found an apartment or house, this would be a wonderful spell to perform a day or two before moving in.

YOU WILL NEED
Cleansing and protection incense, such as white sage
A love incense of your choice

WHAT TO DO

Enter your new apartment together before you bring any of your belongings into it. Light the cleansing and protection incense, allowing it to smoke.

Travel together slowly *deosil* (clockwise), starting at the front door. Move into each room and smudge every corner, closet, attic, basement, window, etc. In other words, keep your incense smoking, and wave it into all of the spaces you want to smudge. You may have a ritual fan or wing (properly cleansed and dedicated, of course) that you use to help waft the smoke where you want it to go, or you can use your hand.

As you travel through the rooms together, recite the following, taking alternate turns: "God and Goddess, with Your help we release any negativity that might linger here."

When you have returned back to the front door, say together: "Thank You, God and Goddess, for releasing all negativity from our new home. For this we give thanks. . . . And so it is! Blessed be!"

Next you will want to fill the rooms with protection, love, compassion, and, quite possibly, lust.

Light the love incense of your choice and slowly follow the same pattern, reciting the following repeatedly, taking turns: "God and Goddess, fill our new home with protection, love, and the eternal bond of commitment."

When you have returned to the front door, say together: "Thank You, God and Goddess, for filling our new home with protection, love, and eternal commitment. For this we give thanks. . . . And so it is! Blessed be!"

Now you can let whatever incense is left burn in the center of your living room while you hug and kiss.

—Love Consummation Spell—

This ritual is a lovely way to consummate the marriage. This ritual must be entered into with free will on the part of both of you, and could prove to be just the thing to privately celebrate your marriage. This is a very personal, private, and spiritual union that you will share only with the God and Goddess. On a side note, this spell is a powerful romantic and sexual spell, and is best performed on your wedding night.

YOU WILL NEED

Essential oil of your choice, associated with love
Incense of your choice, associated with love
Red rose petals
A red taper candle
Four quarter candles (green for North, blue for East, red for South, purple for West)
A small athame
A bowl of fruit filled with washed and cut strawberries, raspberries, peaches, and pears.
A list of love affirmations such as: "I will always love you, My eyes will never wander, You are beautiful, You are my soul mate, I want you," and so on.

CAST A CIRCLE

First cast a circle for protection. Place the four quarter candles at the edges of the room representing the North, South, East, and West. If you are unsure of where the directions are, check the stars or use a compass. Stand and walk *deosil* together around the perimeter of your circle three times, visualizing an intensely bright white light surrounding and protecting you and your loved one in your sacred space. Now say together, "Our circle is cast. Together we have created sacred space for our protection. As above, so below."

CALL THE QUARTERS

Call the quarters next. I suggest again that you both call the quarters together, to share with them the anticipation you have in consummating your special day. Start at the North and call the quarters in *deosil* order. It is customary to face the quarter that you are calling, and bow to the Spirits when you welcome them.

North

"We call to the North, Spirits of Earth, be with us as the foundation of our life together."

Light the green candle and say, *"Be with us to witness our loving union. Welcome."*

East

"We call to the East, Spirits of Air, be with us as the gentle whisper that tells us we are one."

Light the blue candle and say, *"Be with us to witness our loving union. Welcome."*

South

"We call to the South, Spirits of Fire, be with us as the passion in our union."

Light the red candle and say, *"Be with us to witness our loving union. Welcome."*

West
"We call to the West, Spirits of Water, be with us, as the emotional outpouring we share with one another."

Light the purple candle and say, *"Be with us to witness our loving union. Welcome."*

INVOKE THE GOD AND GODDESS

The quarter candles should be the only source of light in the room. Next, you will invoke the God and Goddess together. You will have no representation for Them. Just know that They are there.

God and Goddess together
"We call to the God and Goddess, the role models for our loving union. Be with us to witness the Great Rite. Welcome."

Scatter the rose petals all over the floor.

SPELLWORK

Using your athame, take turns carving the first name of your partner on the red candle. Then draw a heart around your names the best you can.

Now consecrate your candle with the essential oil that you have chosen. You will do this by taking turns and placing a drop of oil on your finger. Each of you outline the drawn heart with the oil and then say together, "God and Goddess, we now purify this candle so that it may be released of all negativity, that which we can see and that which we cannot, and let it be known that it will be used for love magick. For this we give thanks. And so it is! Blessed be!"

Now sit on the floor facing each other with the unlit candle in front of you and the bowl of fruit and affirmations of love next to you on one side.

Pick up a piece of fruit and feed it to your partner as you recite one of the affirmations, always followed by: "I am one with you forever!"

While your partner is eating slowly take off an article of your clothing. When your partner is done eating the fruit you may kiss across the unlit candle. Alternate feeding and affirming until you do not want any more fruit or you are both skyclad.

Now each of you take a match and light it. Together light the red candle between the two of you and say in unison, "God and Goddess, we are one! For this we give thanks. And so it is! Blessed be!"

Let the candle burn down to the very end, while you gaze into each other eyes in silence through the flame. Try to only look into each other's eyes.

When the candle goes out you may hug, kiss, and practice the Great Rite with the God and Goddess as your witnesses. I suggest a smallish red candle, since you may not want to wait all night for the candle to go down. But not too small. Anticipation is tremendously romantic, and your Great Rite should never be rushed.

RELEASE THE CIRCLE

Now that you have consummated your marriage, you may thank the God and Goddess, release the quarters, and take down the circle.

God and Goddess

"God and Goddess, role models of our loving union, thank You for witnessing the Great Rite. Stay if You will, leave if You must. Blessed be!"

Now release the quarters. Start with the West because that is that last one you called. From there you want to release them *widdershins* (counterclockwise). Bow and extinguish each candle as you dismiss the associated quarter.

West

"Spirits of the West, of Water, thank you for sharing our emotional outpouring. Stay if you will, leave if you must. Blessed be!"

South

"Spirits of the South, of Fire, thank you for the passion in our union. Stay if you will, leave if you must. Blessed be!"

East

"Spirits of the East, of Air, thank you for whispering that we are one. Stay if you will, leave if you must. Blessed be!"

North

"Spirits of the North, of Earth, thank you for being the foundation of our life together. Stay if you will, leave if you must. Blessed be!"

To release the circle itself, walk together around the circle *widdershins*. Visualize that you are releasing the circle, that the bright white light dissipates around you as you go. When you have walked once around the perimeter of the circle, face the altar together and say, "This circle is released, but never broken. Merry meet, merry part, and merry meet again!" Any remaining energy in the circle will linger, like a cherished memory that overspreads your life.

You have just officially united as one flesh, and have embarked on your combined spiritual and physical union together. There is nothing more powerful and magickal than finally experiencing the Great Rite together, after a long and awaited anticipation. Remember always that your union is built on perfect love and perfect trust, from this moment on! Blessed be!

*Food that is blessed with prayer certainly
adds an element of love magick, and changes
the moods and attitudes of everyone sitting at
the table.*

CHAPTER 12

HANDFASTING FEAST

CHOOSING A THEME for your food can be as challenging as every other aspect of your handfasting or wedding day. Many weddings are held at reception halls that will provide you with a choice of menus. Once you choose a menu, all you have to do is sit back and enjoy the day. They will often also provide all of the desserts and even the wedding cake.

If you choose to have your wedding outside of a reception hall with its own catering service, you can hire a private caterer. Remember to keep your choice within your budget. A caterer will give you different meal ideas, let you sample plenty of options, and then when you decide what you want, they will prepare the food, serve your guests, and do all the cleanup. A caterer usually charges per person, not per dish, so your guest count can determine your budget.

Another option for your day, especially if you are having financial challenges, is to have a potluck meal. You can indicate on the invitations when you send them out that you would like that guest to please forgo a gift for you and your partner, and instead to bring a dish to share. You could designate an appetizer, salad, main dish, or dessert for each invitation. The best part about "potluck" is knowing that all of the food was infused with good wishes as it was being prepared and that magick was baked right into it. Witch or no Witch, every cook fills her favorite dishes with plenty of love.

Blessing the Food

In the case of a function hall or caterer preparing the food, where you are relying on a complete stranger to prepare the food, you might want to ask your chosen officiant to make a trip to the kitchen and say a cleansing blessing and prayer over all of the food. This way you will know that by the time your guests receive theirs it will be cleared of negativity and infused with the love of the God and Goddess. You may also want to ask your chosen officiant if they can say a blessing for the food and the drink once everyone is served.

It is traditional in my family to begin eating before we say the blessing over the food. Because we all have crazy schedules, it is amazing that we can even manage to sit down and have a family meal every evening, and we are far too hungry to look at our plates waiting for a prayer. So I allow everyone to take a couple of bites before reciting the prayer, which we say all together. I marvel at how different the food tastes before and after we say the prayer, and how much better it tastes after the prayer. Food that is blessed with prayer certainly adds an element of love magick, and changes the moods and attitudes of everyone sitting at the table.

The prayer we use was written by Silver RavenWolf but our family added some personal touches to the end to make it our own. Here's the prayer we use—feel free to incorporate this into the prayer that you use for your handfasting food:

"The table round contains the earth and thus becomes the Mother, we share Her bounty in this hour and bless and love each other. So Mote It Be! It's a Good Life! I can! I will! I believe! Thank You, God and Goddess."

Wedding Food from Around the World

Below you will find some meal ideas based on specific wedding traditions from around the world that Pagan couples whom I have spoken with chose to use in their handfasting. In my experience, the cultures listed below are the most common ones combined with Paganism in an interfaith couple. If you are an interfaith couple and want to incorporate traditions from a religion or region not listed here, you can search the Internet for other traditional wedding foods—or just ask Grandma! Feel free to incorporate any aspects that sound delicious or special in some way to you and your partner.

Irish Wedding Food

The food served at an Irish wedding is exactly what you might expect: corned beef and cabbage with Irish soda bread and mead or beer. The Irish wedding cake is a fruitcake soaked in Irish whiskey.

Italian Wedding Food

Italian weddings are extremely generous and extravagant, and include more food than the guests could possibly eat. It would not be unusual to see a twelve-course meal at an Italian wedding. It would begin with appetizers ranging from stuffed mushrooms, prosciutto, an olive bar, salami, all the way to fried calamari. Next you would be tempted with several pasta dishes, salads, and all kinds of exotic meats. The list is comprehensive and incredible. You get the idea, but it is important to mention that fried dough twists and wedding candy are always served at an Italian wedding to ensure good luck for the new couple. Also, there is not always a wedding cake at an Italian wedding; instead there is a "union of bitter and sweet" where sugared almonds are served.

Japanese Wedding Food

At a Japanese wedding it is likely that you will be served the following foods: tai, or sea bream, served raw or salted on the grill; kombu, or kelp, that will be served in the form of soup, or rolled and simmered; kazunoko, or herring roe, in order to promote fertility for the new couple; and sekihan, red azuki beans and rice, because red is such an important color in a Japanese wedding.

Chinese Wedding Food

In China the number eight is a lucky number, so a Chinese wedding meal would consist of eight courses. It is not unusual to be served during this eight-course meal the food of an animal that chooses a mate for life, such as the duck, in order to ensure that the marriage lasts for life. The meal might actually be Peking duck, because it is red, a color sacred to weddings in China. The Chinese wedding cake is called the "Dragon and Phoenix" cake, because the dragon and phoenix symbolize the yin and yang or balance of male and female energies.

Jewish Wedding Food

In a traditional Jewish wedding the meal would be kosher, but because this is an interfaith marriage, that would probably not be the case. Jewish weddings also provide more food than anyone could possibly eat, sometimes as a special show of family pride and hospitality. Along with the traditional beef or lamb dish served with potatoes and vegetables, it would not be unusual to have stations serving all kinds of meats carved from the bone, and several exotic Jewish Mediterranean offerings. This might include gefilte fish, smoked salmon, herring, chopped liver and crackers, tzimmes, knishes, potato latkes, and kugel, an egg noodle pudding. There would be plenty of challah bread, and for dessert you would find hamantashen (pastry with fruit in the middle) and mandlebread (hard wafers with fruit and nuts throughout). These might be somewhere on the massive dessert table, with the wedding cake elegantly displayed in the middle.

Muslim Wedding Food

Muslims do not eat pork or drink alcohol, so you will not see either of these served at a Muslim wedding, but their food is rich and heavy so you are not likely to forget it quickly. You will see biryani, a rice and lamb dish, or shami, which is a meat and lentil kabob served with aloo ki takaree, a potato curry. For dessert, the wedding cake will be nothing less than extravagant and on display on its own table.

Hindu Wedding Food

At the Hindu wedding, the food is the most important aspect of the whole wedding. There is nothing cooked with onion or garlic, and usually the meal is strictly vegetarian. You will find puris, which is an Indian flat bread, rice, vegetables cooked in coconut sauce, beans, yams, and chutney. For dessert, shrikhand, which is strained yogurt; basundi, which is creamy milk pudding; and a dairy-based drink called mattha will be served. Traditional Hindu wedding feasts do not include wedding cakes; vida, or sweet paan, will be served instead.

Buddhist Wedding Food

At a Buddhist wedding you would find steamed rice with roasted beef or pork, accompanied by fried and stewed foods like dal makhani, naan, and paneer. It wouldn't be a Buddhist wedding without nettle soup made from orchid flowers, and cottage cheese with cooked bamboo sticks. The desserts will include gajar ka halwa, a carrot pudding, and gulab jamun, sweet balls of dough fried in a flavored sugar syrup. There may or may not be a wedding cake.

Tips for Food Choice and Presentation

Food is an integral part of the wedding day. You may find yourself having a difficult time deciding on just the right menu to please everyone. Remember these few simple steps to make a lasting impression on this special day's feast:

+ Keeping the food theme consistent with the theme and culture of your wedding will provide your senses with another avenue of personal and interpersonal connection, which will enhance the overall experience quite nicely.
+ A prayer over the food will infuse your cuisine with love, the most underrated aspect of preparing delicious food today. Taste the difference of your own food when prepared hastily and under stressful conditions versus when cooking big meals that you can make a labor of love.
+ Include vegetarian and nonalcoholic choices in your menu. Even though you may not be able to account for every allergy and dietary idiosyncrasy, having healthier choices will help those guests who are normally in the minority, and will also promote better choices for all the guests. You don't want people to think that the only theme is drinking heavily and eating badly.
+ Be creative. Sometimes creative presentations of food make longer-lasting impressions than the food itself. Cascading shrimp over an ice sculpture, having animal-shaped fruit baskets, colorful hors d'oeuvres and vegetables, and champagne fountains are all ways to add a little sizzle to the most memorable day of your lives.

Regardless of whether your guests prepare a potluck dinner, you cook the food yourself, or you hire a caterer, be sure that in all the excitement you don't miss out on the food. Bon appétit!

*With this handfasting ribbon, you are
bound in perfect love and perfect trust,
for as long as you both shall live.*

CHAPTER 13

SAMPLE RITUALS, PRAYERS, AND IDEAS

THE SPIRITUAL UNION of two people, in deep love and admiration for one another, is one of the most incredible experiences I have ever seen on this physical plane of existence. I have been given a calling to serve the children of the God and Goddess, and being able to officiate so many of these unions is one of the treasured gifts I have received in return for my life's work. It never ceases to amaze me how the most beautiful things in this life seem to be those events that also cause time to stand still, touching eternity, so that they can be seen and enjoyed at all of the levels of our existence.

This chapter includes several sample rituals, with prayers and additional ideas, to help you and your loved one formulate exactly how you want to orchestrate your commitment to one another. Read through this chapter and spend some time with the God and Goddess before choosing elements for your ceremony, or writing your own. Meditate, and the Truth will be revealed to you.

Consecration and Dedication

Before the ceremony, the high priestess will bless, consecrate, or dedicate all of the items on the altar. Please remember to do them in the proper order according to your tradition, and do not forget or ignore this step in the ritual process. The last thing that you and your partner want is to have your wedding influenced by any negativity coming from your consumable items or ritual tools.

If you have picked a particular God and Goddess from Chapter 2, inform the high priestess before she begins, and she will replace the words *God* and *Goddess* with Their names.

Instructions for a Pagan Handfasting Ritual

This ritual can be performed singly by a high priestess or a high priest. If you belong to a coven where you have both a high priestess and a high priest, then you can make adjustments to have it fit your individual needs. For example, the high priestess can perform the duties for the bride and the high priest can perform the duties for the groom. The ritual below is written as though you only have a high priestess.

For a Pagan handfasting you should cast a circle. The circle is where you are protected in sacred space, and it creates an area outside place and time. As a couple, you want to make sure that your union is protected from all negativity, ensuring that you begin your new life together in a positive direction.

Before beginning, you will want to have the area you'll be using for your handfasting well prepared. You can place chairs around the perimeter of your circle so that any guests who cannot stand will have a place to sit. In this ritual we will assume that you have a total of eight attendants: a bridesmaid and an usher at each quarter. Certainly, this ritual can be adjusted to your needs. Be sure to leave two open spaces at each quarter. This is where your bridesmaids and ushers will stand. The rest of the guests can stand behind the chairs.

Set the altar in the center of the circle, facing the North quarter, leaving enough room for the officiant and the wedding party to stand in front of it inside the circle of chairs, with the maid of honor slightly behind and next to the bride, and the best man slightly behind and next to the bridegroom. If you have a flower girl and ring-bearer, be sure that they can comfortably fit behind everyone in the circle. Parents of the bride and bridegroom can stand on the East and West sides of the altar, facing it. This formation will form a semi-circle or crescent moon shape inside the circle. Be sure that the high priestess can stand either in front of the wedding party or on the opposite side of the altar facing South, looking at you and your partner.

Before the ritual begins, have the high priestess smudge the area, sweep away any negativity from the ritual circle, and consecrate or anoint the flowers and the wedding party outside the circle.

FOR YOUR ALTAR YOU WILL NEED

One silver candle (representing the Goddess)
One gold candle (representing the God)
Candles for the four quarters (directions):
   A green candle (representing North)
   A blue candle (representing East)
   A red candle (representing South)
   A purple candle (representing West)
A small bowl of salt representing earth
Incense representing air
Another red or orange candle representing fire
A small bowl of water representing water
Your choice of an anointing or dedication essential oil
Handfasting ribbon
A chalice with grape juice or wine
An athame
A piece of bread on a small plate
Matches
A candle extinguisher
A besom (place next to altar)

SET UP ALTAR

Place your Goddess candle at the upper left-hand corner of your rectangular altar and the God candle at the upper right. Place the four quarter candles at the center of each side of your altar representing the North, South, East, and West. If you are unsure of where the directions are in relation to your altar, use a compass. Now place the representations of the elements (earth, air, fire, and water) just inside the quarter candles. Place your handfasting ribbon in the middle of the altar, your chalice of wine close to the Goddess candle, your athame close to the God candle, and your bread near the wine. Your ring-bearer will have the rings. If you do not have a ring-bearer, the rings can be held by the best man and maid of honor.

PROCESSIONAL

The number of guests you are inviting and the number of people in your wedding party will determine the size of your circle. Let us assume that you will require space inside the circle of guests to have a maid of honor standing next to the bride, a best man standing next to the bridegroom, four bridesmaids, four ushers, a flower girl, a ring-bearer, and parents on either side.

Be sure to leave a walkway on the outside of the circle where the South quarter is. You can lay down a red carpet, if you like. You can have any music that you want, even the wedding march if you desire. Have everyone in the wedding party enter the circle from the South in a procession. The high priestess will be waiting inside the circle of guests. First the groom will be escorted into the circle by both the best man and the maid of honor, one on each side. The groom and the best man will take their places on the right-hand side of the altar. The maid of honor will take her place on the left-hand side of the altar. Next the parents of the bride-groom, then the parents of the bride will enter the circle. They will all take their appropriate places in the semicircle before the altar. The bridesmaids and the ushers will enter the circle in pairs, but will divide to each side of the circle, bridesmaids on the right and ushers on the left, leaving room for the bride to enter.

The bride will then walk into and through the center of the circle alone, with the ring-bearer and flower girl side by side behind her, the flower girl casting flowers on both sides of the path. The ring-bearer and flower girl will stand at the North quarter of the circle and the bride will take her place in front of the altar on the left-hand side.

CAST THE CIRCLE

Once the wedding party is in the circle of guests and the tools and supplies have been prepared, the protective circle is now cast. The high priestess and the wedding party can all join in casting the circle. First the high priestess picks up the water from the altar and sprinkles salt into it, and then hands it to the best man to carry around the circle for the first pass. The best man will start in the North and travel *deosil* (clockwise), sprinkling the water and salt mix on the perimeter of the circle with his fingers. The high priestess replaces the water on the altar and picks up the incense. She hands it to the maid of honor, who also starts in the North and travels *deosil*, being sure that the smoke covers the perimeter of the circle. Next, the bridesmaids and the ushers will pair off and each pair will stand in an assigned quarter. When they get the signal from the high priestess, they will walk in pairs, *deosil* from the quarter they are in, all the way around the circle, ending at the quarter that they began in. While walking, they will visualize an intensely bright white light surrounding and protecting you and your loved ones in your sacred space. As this is happening, the flower girl will sprinkle some fresh flower petals on the altar.

When the circle is cast, the high priestess says:

With the magick of perfect love and perfect trust, this circle is cast. Ladies and gentlemen, we are gathered here [tonight] [today] to witness the spiritual union, the handfasting, of [names of bride and bridegroom] in the presence of the God and Goddess.

CALL THE QUARTERS

The **HIGH PRIESTESS** will now say:

We will now call upon the guardians of the quarters. I ask that everyone please be respectful and face the quarter that is being called.

The **HIGH PRIESTESS** asks everyone to face North:

We call to the spirits of North, of earth, to enfold you in a solid foundation. Be with us this night.

Have the bridesmaid in the North quarter come up and light the (green) North candle. As she does, **EVERYONE** repeats:

Be with us this night.

The **HIGH PRIESTESS** asks everyone to face East:

We call to the spirits of East, of air, to breathe new life into you each and every day. Be with us this night.

Have the bridesmaid in the East quarter come up and light the (blue) East candle. As she does, **EVERYONE** repeats:

Be with us this night.

The **HIGH PRIESTESS** asks everyone to face South:

We call to the spirits of South, of fire, to bring you everlasting passion in this loving union. Be with us this night.

Have the bridesmaid in the South quarter come up and light the (red) South candle. As she does, **EVERYONE** repeats:

Be with us this night.

The **HIGH PRIESTESS** asks everyone to face West:
We call to the spirits of West, of water, as the loving emotion that flows from your souls. Be with us this night.

Have the bridesmaid in the West quarter come up and light the (purple) West candle. As she does, **EVERYONE** repeats:
Be with us this night.

INVOKE THE GOD AND GODDESS

The **BEST MAN** and **MAID OF HONOR** invoke the God and Goddess respectively.

God

We call to the God, with all of your strength and stamina. Come to us with your lessons of longevity and be with us through all of eternity. Be with us this night.

As the person invoking the God lights the God candle, **EVERYONE** repeats:
Be with us this night.

Goddess

We call to the Goddess, with all of your love and compassion. Come to us with your lessons of faithfulness. Be with us this night.

As the person invoking the Goddess lights the Goddess candle, **EVERYONE** repeats:
Be with us this night.

The **HIGH PRIESTESS** then says:
God and Goddess and spirits of the North, South, East, and West, this bride and groom have asked you here to witness their spiritual union. They ask that you look upon them and bless them as they are

bound to one another in perfect love and perfect trust. Friends and family who are present here tonight, [bride and bridegroom's names] have asked you here to witness their spiritual union.

DECLARATION OF FREE WILL

Could you both please state your names in full before the God and Goddess, so that they might know you and smile upon your union.

The groom states his name, followed by the bride.

The **HIGH PRIESTESS** asks:
Do you both come here to be handfasted to one another of your own free will?
The **BRIDE** and **GROOM** reply:
We do.

The **HIGH PRIESTESS** says:
[Bride] and [groom], you both stand before me asking that the God and Goddess hear your vows of love and commitment to one another, so I ask that you face one another and make your vows.

EXCHANGE VOWS

The **GROOM** begins, holding the ring at the tip of the bride's ring finger. You may write your own vows to be said here, or use the following:

I, [bridegroom's name] come here of my own free will to handfast my beloved [bride's name]. I wish for our minds, souls, and bodies to unite and become one flesh. I will take care of you, [bride's name], as though my own life depended on it. I will cherish you always, and remember that you are a gift given to me from the Gods. May the God and Goddess keep me sincere and faithful to my vows now, always, and forever. For this I give thanks. And so it is! Blessed be!

The groom places the ring on the bride's finger.

The **BRIDE** then makes her vows, holding the ring at the tip of the groom's ring finger. Again, you may write your own vows, or use the following:

I, [bride's name] come here of my own free will to handfast my beloved [bridegroom's name]. I wish for our minds, souls, and bodies to unite and become one flesh. I will take care of you, [bridegroom's name], as though my own life depended on it. I will cherish you always, and remember that you are a gift given to me from the Gods. May the God and Goddess keep me sincere and faithful to my vows now, always, and forever. For this I give thanks. And so it is! Blessed be!

Place the ring on the bridegroom's finger.

ANOINTING

The **HIGH PRIESTESS** now anoints the bride with the essential oil by drawing a pentacle on her body, touching the right hip, the forehead, the left hip, the right shoulder, the left shoulder, and back to the right hip while saying:

[Bride's name], child of the God and Goddess, I charge and dedicate you to serve the God and Goddess in whatever capacity They see fit in your spiritual union. So mote it be!

The **HIGH PRIESTESS** then anoints the bridegroom with the essential oil by drawing a pentacle on his body, touching the right hip, the forehead, the left hip, the right shoulder, the left shoulder, and back to the right hip while saying:

[Bridegroom's name], child of the God and Goddess, I charge and dedicate you to serve the God and Goddess in whatever capacity They see fit in your spiritual union. So mote it be!

The **HIGH PRIESTESS** will now say:
Because it is unethical to perform magick on anyone else's behalf without their permission, we will now ask the bride and groom if they would like us to perform loving magick for them. I ask you [bride's name and groom's name], would you like us to perform loving magick on your behalf?

The **BRIDE** and **GROOM** reply:
We do.

The **HIGH PRIESTESS** says:
We will now perform a loving, lasting magick for the bride and groom, ensuring their successful lifelong union together.

The **HIGH PRIESTESS** then leads everyone in raising a cone of power with the chant of your choice. The **HIGH PRIESTESS** monitors the energy until it has peaked and then signals everyone to direct the energy to the bride and bridegroom.

THE GREAT RITE

In preparation for the symbolic Great Rite, the **HIGH PRIESTESS** says:
I will now ask the bridegroom to lift the bride's veil.

The bridegroom will lift the veil very carefully and slowly, as though it were a spiritual revelation. The **HIGH PRIESTESS** hands the chalice of wine to the bride and the athame to the bridegroom, and says:

There is nothing more magickal and spiritually intense than the physical embracing of two people. Pagans believe that there is no better way to transcend the physical and experience the divine within, than by sharing in sexual union. The physical and the spiritual planes are equally important to a Pagan. By performing this symbolic rite, you are experiencing both the physical and the spiritual at the same time. There is no room for shame here, only mutual respect. I now ask [bride and bridegroom's names] to share this physical and spiritual union with all of us who are present here tonight, and in the eyes of the God and Goddess.

The bridegroom slowly lowers the athame into the chalice. When he removes it, let the wine drip several times into the chalice before placing the athame back on the altar. The bride will hand the chalice to the **HIGH PRIESTESS**, who says:

This union marks the blood and body of the God and Goddess uniting as one, and [bride's name and bridegroom's name] have now united together as One.

HANDFASTING

In preparation for the actual handfasting, the **HIGH PRIEST-ESS** says:

I ask that [bride and bridegroom's names] now face each other and join hands, left hand to left hand and right hand to right hand.

The **HIGH PRIESTESS** picks up the handfasting ribbon and fastens it in a figure eight around the couple's hands, tying it three times at the bottom, and says:

You are now bound as one in the eyes of the God and Goddess and with this handfasting ribbon you are bound by the knot of the triple Goddess, until physical death do you part. (Or "for as long as the love shall last.")

The **HIGH PRIESTESS** then lifts the chalice with the wine in it. With her hand over the top she says:

God and Goddess, You hold the secret to the mysteries. I ask You to bless this wine, the blood of the Goddess, and bring with it Your blessings of health, wealth, peace, and eternal happiness to this newly handfasted couple. Blessed be!

The high priestess hands the chalice to the maid of honor, who will not drink, but instead will serve it to the bridegroom, and then hand it to the best man, who will not drink, but instead will serve it to the bride, and then the maid of honor will place it back on the altar.

The **HIGH PRIESTESS** lifts the bread and holds her hand over it, saying:

God and Goddess, You hold the secret to the mysteries. I ask You to bless this bread, the body of the God, and bring with it Your blessings of health, wealth, peace, and eternal happiness to this newly handfasted couple. Blessed be!

The high priestess hands the bread to the maid of honor, who will feed it to the bridegroom, and then hand it to the best man, who will feed it to the bride, and then the maid of honor will place it back on the altar.

The HIGH PRIESTESS then dips the bread into the chalice, and places it back on the plate as an offering to the God and Goddess, saying:

God and Goddess, please accept this offering given in perfect love and perfect trust from us to You. Blessed be!

JUMPING THE BESOM

Now comes the fun of jumping the besom. The best part about having the couple jump the besom is that they need to do it with the handfasting ribbon still binding them. It can be a challenge, and it is so much fun for everyone to watch.

The high priestess hands the besom to the best man, who will hold one end; the maid of honor will hold the other. They must hold it steady, about six inches off the ground. Then the HIGH PRIESTESS encourages the bride and bride-groom to jump over the besom:

I now ask [bride's name and bridegroom's name] to jump over the besom, once for their union and as many times after that for the number of children they would like.

Bride and bridegroom jump over the besom. The HIGH PRIESTESS then says:

It is now time to thank the God and Goddess and dismiss the quarters.

THANKING THE GOD AND GODDESS

Goddess

To thank the Goddess, the MAID OF HONOR says:

We thank You, Goddess, for infusing all of Your love and compassion in this newly handfasted couple. Your lessons in faithfulness are understood. Stay if You will, go if You must. Blessed be!

As the maid of honor extinguishes the Goddess candle, **EVERYONE** repeats:

Blessed be!

God

To thank the God, the **BEST MAN** says:

We thank You, God, for bringing all of Your strength and stamina. Longevity will be with this newly handfasted couple through all of eternity. Stay if You will, go if You must. Blessed be!

As the best man extinguishes the God candle, **EVERYONE** repeats:

Blessed be!

DISMISSING THE QUARTERS

West

To dismiss the quarters, the **HIGH PRIESTESS** invites everyone to face the West and says:

Thank you, spirits of West, of water. Your loving emotion flows deep in the souls of this newly handfasted couple. Stay if you will, go if you must. Blessed be!

As the final words are spoken, the usher in the West quarter comes up and extinguishes the (purple) West candle. **EVERYONE** repeats:

Blessed be!

South

The **HIGH PRIESTESS** invites everyone to face South and says:

"Thank you, spirits of South. Your everlasting passion is infused in this newly handfasted couple. Stay if you will, go if you must. Blessed be!

As the final words are spoken, the usher in the South quarter comes up and extinguishes the (red) South candle. **EVERYONE** repeats:

Blessed be!

East

The **HIGH PRIESTESS** invites everyone to face East and says:

Thank you, spirits of East, of air. Your gentle loving whisper will breathe new life every day into this newly handfasted couple. Stay if you will, go if you must. Blessed be!

As the final words are spoken, the usher in the East quarter comes up and extinguishes the (blue) East candle. **EVERYONE** repeats:

Blessed be!

North

The **HIGH PRIESTESS** invites everyone to face North and says:

Thank you, spirits of North, of earth. Your solid foundation and security is only the beginning for this newly handfasted couple. Stay if you will, go if you must. Blessed be!

As the final words are spoken, the usher in the North quarter comes up and extinguishes the (green) North candle. **EVERYONE** repeats:

Blessed be!

RELEASING THE CIRCLE

The bridesmaids and ushers will now walk the circle *widdershins* (counterclockwise) to release it. The **HIGH PRIESTESS** says:

We may have thanked the God and Goddess and dismissed the quarters, but the exchange that has happened here tonight will never be forgotten by Them or us. It is nothing less than magickal. May They live in our hearts always, and may we be shining examples of Their indwelling spirit and love. [Bride's name] and [groom's name], you now may kiss. This circle is released, but never broken. Merry meet, merry part, and merry meet again. Ladies and gentlemen, I now present to you Mr. and Mrs. _____ [or however they wish to be announced]. Blessed be!

The guests may cheer or applaud. The **HIGH PRIESTESS** says:

The bride and bridegroom may now remove their handfasting ribbon by wriggling their hands out of it. It is bad luck to cut the ribbon.

When the bride and groom have freed themselves from the handfasting ribbon, the wedding party leaves the circle in the following order: bride and groom; flower girl and ring-bearer; maid of honor and best man; parents of the bride; parents of the groom; bridesmaids and ushers; priestess.

Pagan Interfaith Marriage Options

If your marriage is interfaith, you might want a nondenominational theme, with undertones of Paganism and the other tradition. If you are going to combine traditions, you need to be equally respectful of both faiths. Remember that as Pagans, we do not mix pantheons, as it is highly disrespectful. Why not show that same respect to people of other faiths? Certainly different religious beliefs can be incorporated together without either faith feeling dominated or rejected.

You should not cast a circle or invoke the God and Goddess for an interfaith ceremony, because it could prove to be uncomfortable for people in attendance. You will have to have faith that They, the God and Goddess, are forever with you. For purposes of saving time and space in this chapter, I will describe the different parts of the ceremony, but will leave out the processionals and recessionals. You and your fiancé can decide how you would like that to work in a way that is comfortable for both of you.

In a Pagan interfaith ceremony, the setup will be the same regardless of the other faith. The bride and bridegroom will be in the ceremonial area, with the bride on the left, the groom on the right facing the officiant, and the chosen officiant in front of them. You will have a small table or altar between you and the officiant, or you can place it off to one side. Once you pick the elements of the ceremony you want, you will want to have all the necessary items on your table. If you would like to have your chosen officiant smudge the room and consecrate the items, you should be sure that it is okay with your fiancé. Then have the officiant do it before the event begins.

Pagan Interfaith Ceremony Aspects

Below are options for your interfaith wedding ceremony. Mix and combine them any way you like to design the interfaith wedding of your dreams. Depending on what denomination your partner is, you can easily change things around in any fashion necessary to accommodate your needs.

—————Gathering Words—————

NONDENOMINATIONAL GATHERING WORDS

OFFICIANT: *"Good evening, and welcome to the joyous occasion of this couple's marriage. I ask that you please leave the concerns of your everyday world behind you, and join me in celebrating their marriage.*

"[Bride's name and bridegroom's name], your marriage tonight will be publicly, legally, and spiritually recognized. The vows you will exchange tonight will profess your heartfelt union with one another so that you may join as soul mates as you face this world together, hand in hand.

"Marriage is an act of free will, and to remain as one you will need to renew your vows of love each and every day, especially as life's challenges arise. Those of us who are already married, please take a moment to tell your partner that you are still committed to your relationship.

"[Bride's name and bridegroom's name] are committing themselves to each other tonight in perfect love and perfect trust. They are committing to work through conflict as well as enjoy peace, to work hard to provide for one another as well as play together, to struggle through hardship and coast through the easy times, to give all of themselves to one another as well as to receive, and to be the very best of friends."

Now you might want to ask the ushers or bridesmaids to bring the salt, water, incense, and candle, and place it on the table as you bless the four directions. Note that you will be asking the elements for their blessings, not calling the spirits of the quarters, because doing so would be highly disrespectful to your partner's faith.

—*Mid-Ceremony*—

PAGAN-STYLE BLESSINGS TO THE FOUR DIRECTIONS

OFFICIANT: *"It was believed in ancient times that the elements of our Universe bring with them special gifts. Tonight, in preserving that old tradition, we will ask that these gifts be given to this couple.*

"We bless this marriage with the gifts from the North. From the North comes the gift of earth, symbolizing a solid foundation to build your loving union. We bless this marriage with gifts from the East. From the East comes air, our incense, symbolizing the gift of communication between you, and the wisdom of knowing when to be silent and listen. We bless this marriage with gifts from the South. From the South comes the spark of passion, our candle, symbolizing a warm and welcoming hearth. We bless this marriage with gifts from the West, our water. From the West comes the sharing of heartfelt emotions that flow as the river of life.

"May you always remember these gifts that have been given to you in order to help ensure your successful marriage together."

JEWISH CHUPAH CEREMONY

OFFICIANT: *"In the Jewish faith, the chupah represents the bond of love and the promise of beginning your spiritual union in your new* *home. The shelter of your new home will keep you warm even in the coldest of months and most difficult times. May you find peace in your new home and forever use it as your safe haven and source of warmth, comfort, and security.*

"Blessed are You, Lord, our G-d, King of the universe, who has kept us alive, sustained us, and enabled us to reach this season.

Baruch ata Adonai,
El-o-hey-nu mel-ech ha-o-lam,
Sheh-heh-Cheh-ya-nu, v'ki-y'ma-nu,
V'higi-a-nu la-z'man ha-zeh. Amen."

NONDENOMINATIONAL CHARGE TO COUPLE

OFFICIANT: *"More often than not, people believe that couples who come from different religious backgrounds are fighting an uphill battle. [Bride's name and bridegroom's name] feel very differently about this.*

"In reality all marriages are mixed marriages. They are mixed in many respects. Most couples do not spend money the same way, engage in the same line of work, or even argue the same way. Couples who have different religious beliefs are ahead of the game, in that they already know one major difference between them and have already learned how to respect each other. Respect for each other is a key factor in a successful marriage. I ask you, [bride's name and groom's name], to always remember the respect you must give to one another and ask you to continually uphold that responsibility. It takes very compassionate people to appreciate the differences of others—compassionate people like the two of you."

If you would like to include the lighting of the unity candle, you will need to place three candles on your table horizontally in the center. Also, be sure to place matches on the table. Be sure that the colors of the outside candles match your wedding theme; the inside candle should be pure white.

UNITY CANDLE LIGHTING

OFFICIANT: *"Fire is a symbol of passion, and of security in the home. We burn this flame first as an individual within the very core of our being, but then when we meet the person we want to share that love and passion with for the rest of our lives, we join and burn each flame as one.*

"[Bride's name and bridegroom's name], please light the outer candles, representing your individual flames.

"And now, please light the center candle together using the outside candles, representing your intertwined internal flames. May this be the beginning of a passion that grows stronger with each passing day."

Here is where you would place a reading or prayer, depending upon which faith your partner is. Feel free to use any one you like.

—————————————*Readings*—————————————

NONDENOMINATIONAL READING

OFFICIANT: *"Dearest God, love is one of Your richest and greatest gifts to the world. Love between a man and woman which matures into marriage is one of Your most beautiful types of loves. Today, we celebrate that love. May Your blessing be on this wedding service. Protect, guide, and bless [bride's name and bridegroom's name] in their marriage. Surround them and us with Your love, now and always. Amen and Blessed Be."*

PAGAN READING

OFFICIANT: *"I who am the beauty of the green earth, and the white moon among the stars, and the mystery of the waters, I call upon your soul to rise and come unto Me. For I am the soul of nature that gives life unto the universe. From Me all things proceed, and unto Me all things must return. Let My worship be in the heart that rejoices, for all acts of love and pleasure are My rituals."* (Doreen Valiente's *"Charge of the Goddess"*)

JEWISH READING

OFFICIANT: *". . . the LORD G-d caused the man to fall into a deep sleep; and while he was sleeping, he took one of the man's ribs and closed up the place with flesh. Then the LORD G-d made a woman from the rib he had taken out of the man, and he brought her to the man.*

"The man said, "This is now bone of my bones and flesh of my flesh; she shall be called 'woman,' for she was taken out of man." For this reason a man will leave his father and mother and be united to his wife, and they will become one flesh. (Genesis 2:21–24) Amen."

CHRISTIAN READING

OFFICIANT: *"If I speak in the tongues of men and of angels, but have not love, I am only a resounding gong or a clanging cymbal. If I have the gift of prophecy and can fathom all mysteries and all knowledge, and if I have a faith that can move mountains, but have not love, I am nothing. If I give all I possess to the poor and surrender my body to the flames, but have not love, I gain nothing. Love is patient, love is kind. It does not envy, it does not boast, it is not proud. It is not rude, it is not self-seeking, it is not easily angered, it keeps no record of wrongs. Love does not delight in evil but rejoices with* *the truth. It always protects, always trusts, always hopes, always perseveres. Love never fails." (1 Corinthians 13:1–8)*

"And now these three remain: faith, hope and love. But the greatest of these is love. (1 Corinthians 13:13) Amen."

MUSLIM READING

OFFICIANT: *"Lord, grant us in our wives and our offspring the joy of our eyes . . . rewarded with higher places because we are patient, and are met therein with greetings and salutation." (Holy Qur'an 25:74–75)*

HINDU READING

OFFICIANT: *"'A person who finds God in all people will feel their pleasure and pain as his own. The best type of yogi is he who feels for others, whether in grief or pleasure, even as he feels for himself.' (Bhagavad Gita 6:32) May you feel in your partner both of life's pains and pleasures. Aum Tat Sat."* There is no literal translation for the words Aum Tat Sat. Aum means that humans are both physical and spiritual beings, while Tat means "that" and Sat means "truth." But all Hindus know that it is a loving, spiritual way of saying hello or goodbye.

———————— *Wine Ceremonies* ————————

NONDENOMINATIONAL WINE CEREMONY

For this wine ceremony, the officiant will pick up the wine glass from the altar and hand it to the groom to drink. The groom will then hand it to the bride to drink. She will then hand it to the officiant to place back on the altar.

OFFICIANT: *"Wine is the symbol of sweetness and also of bitterness. At times this wine glass will hold sweet joys and happiness that life can bring. Other times it will hold sadness and pain. When you drink from this glass together you are acknowledging that every marriage brings with it the joys and also the sorrows of life."*

THE JEWISH WINE CEREMONY

A Jewish wine ceremony would be the same as the above, but would end with the following:

OFFICIANT would continue: *"Ba-ruch a-ta Adonai, El-o-hey-nu mel-lech-ha-o-lam, Bo-ray pri ha-ga-fen. We praise you, Eternal G-d, Sovereign of the Universe, Creator of the fruit of the vine."*

PAGAN CAKES AND ALE CEREMONY
FOR AN INTERFAITH CEREMONY

The officiant will lift the glass of wine and place a hand over the top.

OFFICIANT: *"Source of All Life [or God and Goddess, if none will be offended], you hold the secret to the mysteries. I ask you to bless this wine, and bring with it your blessings of health, wealth, peace, and eternal happiness to this couple. Blessed be!"*

Then the officiant will hand the wine glass to the maid of honor, who will serve it to the bridegroom, then hand it to the best man, who will serve it to the bride, and then the best man will place it back on the altar or table.

The officiant will lift the bread and place a hand over it.

OFFICIANT: *"Source of All Life, you hold the secret to the mysteries. I ask you to bless this bread, and bring with it your blessings of health, wealth, peace, and eternal happiness to this couple. Blessed be!"*

Then the officiant will hand the bread to the maid of honor, who will feed it to the bridegroom, and then hand it to the best man, who will feed it to the bride, and then the best man will place it back on the altar.

────────── *The Exchanging of Vows* ──────────

EXCHANGING VOWS

Here is where you will exchange your vows. For an interfaith or nondenominational wedding, I would suggest that you write your own. It would be quite loving for you to acknowledge each other's personal faith, and your willingness to support one another down your individual spiritual paths. I have included two samples that you can use, or use as a guide.

EXCHANGING OF VOWS WITH RINGS

The bridegroom will take the ring from the altar, table, or ring-bearer and hold it at the tip of the bride's ring finger as he speaks: *"I, [bridegroom's name], take you, [bride's name], to be my lawfully wedded wife. I promise to share with you all that I have, and all that I am. I promise to support you in all of life's challenges and triumphs and I promise to respect and support your spiritual belief in _____ [here he would name the bride's choice of faith]. For now, always, and as long as we both shall live."*

Then the bridegroom places the ring all the way onto the bride's finger. Then the bride will take the bridegroom's ring and hold it at the tip of his ring finger as she says, *"I, [bride's name], take you, [bridegroom's name], to be my lawfully wedded husband. I promise to share with you all that I have and all that I am.*

I promise to support you in all of life's challenges and triumphs, and I promise to respect and support your spiritual belief in _____ [here she would name the bridegroom's choice of faith]. For now, always, and as long as we both shall live."

Then she would place the ring all the way onto the bridegroom's ring finger.

WESTERN TRADITIONAL CIVIL VOW

OFFICIANT: *"Do you, [bridegroom's name], take [bride's name] to be your lawfully wedded wife, from this day forward, to have and to hold, for better, for worse, for richer and for poorer, in sickness and in health, to love and to cherish, as long as you both shall live?"*

BRIDEGROOM: *"I do."*

OFFICIANT: *"As you place the ring on [bride's name]'s finger, please repeat after me: 'With this ring, I thee wed.'"*

The bridegroom repeats the vow, and puts the ring all the way onto the bride's finger.

OFFICIANT: *"Do you, [bride's name], take [bridegroom's name] to be your lawfully wedded husband, from this day forward, to have and to hold, for better, for worse, for richer and for poorer, in sickness and in health, to love and to cherish, as long as you both shall live?"*

BRIDE: *"I do."*

OFFICIANT: *"As you place the ring on [bridegroom's name]'s finger, please repeat after me: 'With this ring, I thee wed.'"*

The bride repeats the vow, and puts the ring all the way onto the bridegroom's finger.

Optional Extras

PAGAN HANDFASTING CEREMONY
FOR AN INTERFAITH WEDDING

OFFICIANT: *"I ask that [bride and bridegroom's names] now face each other and join hands, left hand to left hand and right hand to right hand."* The officiant will pick up the handfasting ribbon and fasten it in a figure eight around the couple's hands, tying it three times at the bottom. *"You are now bound as one before heaven and earth. With this handfasting ribbon, you are bound in perfect love and perfect trust, for as long as you both shall live."*

BREAKING OF THE GLASS

If your partner is Jewish you can add the traditional breaking of the glass. I have seen more and more couples incorporate this tradition into their interfaith marriage, whether they are Jewish or not. Traditionally this is done by the bridegroom, but I see no reason why the bride and bridegroom couldn't do it together if they wanted to.

OFFICIANT: *"In the Jewish faith it is customary to break a glass at the end of the wedding ceremony. This glass is wrapped in paper and set on the floor for the bridegroom to stomp and break. This glass symbolizes how precious life is and how easily it can be destroyed either physically or in spirit. In all of the joy, we must remember that there is sorrow, and we must work together to support one another."*

The officiant places the wrapped glass on the ground for the bride and bridegroom to stomp. (Some couples use a different glass from the one used in the wine ceremony.) When the glass is firmly and loudly stomped, everyone shouts, *"Mazel tov!"* (Congratulations!)

NONDENOMINATIONAL ENDING PRAYER

OFFICIANT: *"Love is a word that is so difficult to define, and yet we feel it strongly. Love is what brought us all here and love is what will sustain your marriage through the upcoming years. With love all things are possible. I ask that everyone join me in giving our unconditional love and support to this couple, along with our wish that they will have a happy and healthy long life together. Amen, and blessed be!"*

—Benedictions—

NONDENOMINATIONAL BENEDICTION

OFFICIANT: *"Tonight you will travel a new road together. This road has never been traveled by anyone else before; it is unique to the two of you. It is up to you to pay attention to everything that comes your way on this journey. Do not overlook anything or take anything for granted. Additionally, be sure to look ahead at the goals you have laid out together. Dream big, but be sure to cherish every moment you have together."*

CHRISTIAN BENEDICTION

OFFICIANT: *"[A]s God's chosen people, holy and dearly loved, clothe yourselves with compassion, kindness, humility, gentleness and patience. Bear with each other and forgive whatever grievances you may have against one another. Forgive as the Lord forgave you. And over all these virtues put on love, which binds them all together in perfect unity. Let the peace of Christ rule in your hearts, since as members of one body you were called to peace. And be thankful. Amen."* (Colossians 3:12–15)

JEWISH BENEDICTION

OFFICIANT: *"Tonight is the beginning of your new life together. May G-d reach out to you in tenderness, and give you peace. Yi-sa Adonai pa-nav ei-leh-cha v'ya-seim l'cha sha'lom."*

PAGAN BENEDICTION

OFFICIANT: *"May the Spirit of water be with you. May emotion run deep in your souls. May the Spirit of fire be with you. May it stay lit and full of passion. May the Spirit of the Air be with you. May it breathe new life into you every day. May the Spirit of the Earth be with you. May a solid foundation of security enfold you. May Spirit be with you now, always, and forever. For this we give thanks. And so it is! Blessed be!"*

MUSLIM BENEDICTION

OFFICIANT: *"'He created mates for you from yourselves that you might find quiet of mind in them, and he put between you love and compassion.' (Holy Qur'an 30:21) May you always remember these words."*

HINDU BENEDICTION

OFFICIANT: *"We learn from the Bhagavad Gita that the primary purpose of marriage is to have each partner help one another uphold their commitment of divine friendship, love, and loyalty. Aum Tat Sat."*

————Marriage Pronouncement————

OFFICIANT: *"Tonight, [bride's name and bridegroom's name] have asked you here to be a part of their marital union. They have exchanged vows and promises to one another and presented each* *other with wedding rings. They have declared that they will, from this day forward, live a unified life together. It is my pleasure to pronounce them husband and wife. You may now kiss one another. Ladies and Gentlemen, family and friends, it is my pleasure to pres-ent to you, Mr. and Mrs.* _____ [or however they want to be announced]."

As you can see, this format works quite well in design-ing your own interfaith wedding. Simply tell your chosen officiant what parts of the service you would like to incor-porate into your special day and you're done! In your trav-els, if you find other written material in your chosen faith that you would like to incorporate, by all means bring it to your officiant and have it worked into the ceremony. If your partner is of a faith that I have not discussed here, then feel free to take a section of the ceremony and replace it with some meaningful words from that faith. It really isn't dif-ficult planning the ceremony. The problems come the day of the ceremony, because you and your partner will be a bundle of nerves and then you will be glad that this part of your ceremony is in good hands. So choose how you want your ceremony to be, meet with your chosen officiant and let her know what you will be expecting, and then try to relax. It will be over before you know it!

*Feed and water the blossoms of
your love in every way you can.*

CHAPTER 14

THE FIRST YEAR AND A DAY

THE FIRST YEAR OF MARRIAGE is challenging for a new couple. Every couple must face the usual challenges, such as: How will we manage our finances? Who will be responsible for the household chores? How will we spend our free time together? How involved will our in-laws be in our lives? How will we handle conflict? How effectively do we communicate with each other? Being Pagan brings additional challenges to the table. How public or private will we be about our faith? Are we a pair of Solitaires, or can we find Pagan fellowship as a couple, or as a family with children? How will our marriage affect our spiritual growth? Will we continue to grow?

First Year Versus First Year and a Day

Let me first explain why this chapter is titled "The First Year and a Day" and not simply "The First Year." In days of old, the ancients did not adhere to the Gregorian calendar that we know and use today. Our Gregorian calendar consists 223 of twelve months, with each month containing anywhere from twenty-eight to thirty-one days. Perhaps you remember learning some variation of the following: "Thirty days hath September, April, June, and November. All the rest have thirty-one, except February which has twenty-eight and twenty-nine in leap year." When you take the number of days in each month and add them up, you have a total of three hundred and sixty-five days, or one year.

The ancients did not use the Gregorian calendar, but instead used the lunar calendar. Everything was based on the cycles of the moon, and so these ancient peoples would count from one full moon to the next, which would be one month. There were thirteen, a magickal number of full moons or months in a year, but if you add the number of days from one full moon to the next, there are always twenty-eight. If you multiply the thirteen moons by twenty-eight, it equals three hundred and sixty-four.

The Gregorian calendar does a better job (once extra days are added for leap-year) of keeping solar events—equinoxes and solstices—from "drifting" gradually as the years go by. Pagans (and others, perhaps) associate the sun with the male Deity, the God, while the moon is associated with the Goddess, the divine feminine. So a moon year of thirteen months is one day shy of the Gregorian three hundred and sixty-five. We can think of it as Neo-Pagans adding the one day to the three-hundred-and-sixty-four-day lunar year, to equal a Gregorian calendar year of three hundred and sixty-five days. So "a year and a day," Pagan style, is actually one year as we know it in our common calendar. One feminine year, plus one day, meets and matches the masculine year, in perfect balance.

It is still customary today to use the year-and-a-day time frame for study before earning a first, second, or third degree in a coven. Also, this time frame has traditionally been the time period for Pagans to determine whether or not they would choose to stay with their handfasted partner. Pagans believed that if you handfasted for a year and a day, and things didn't work out, you could handpart and look for a new partner. But there is one very important point that seems to have been neglected, or lost in translation over the past two thousand years or so: children.

In ancient Scotland, it was important that a couple could produce offspring. The primary focus was on heterosexual marriages that would bring new life into the world. That being said, it was believed that if a couple could not produce offspring in the first year and a day of marriage, they should part ways and try again with a new partner.

Understand that these people did not know what we know today about medical conditions that can cause infertility. They believed it was simply incompatibility, a sign that the God and Goddess didn't want them together because They prevented the couple from having children. The most important thing to mention here is that if the woman was impregnated or they actually had a child in that first year and a day, there was no option to handpart. They would renew their handfasting in a year and a day and remain together for the rest of their lives, no matter what.

Additionally, if they were handfasted and did not engage in sex in that first year and a day they were still considered legally bound to one another and would marry in the year and a day no matter what. So you can see that the handfasting commitment was not one that was taken as lightly as we might think today.

Handparting

I intentionally have not added a handparting chapter to this book. I am a metaphysician, and believe wholeheartedly in the power of positive thinking and right action. It is far too easy today for people to justify why marriages should split up without putting the necessary time and energy into making them work. No one ever said it was going to be easy, but no one ever said life was easy, either. It is what we make of it. If we live the life of a true Witch, we recognize that no amount of magick is going to change our circumstances until we first take all necessary action on the mundane level of existence. Then we really will have a great chance at succeeding in our marriage. There are cycles in marriage as there are in all of life. There are tides that ebb and flow, sometimes mildly and sometimes with the overwhelming force of a surging sea.

Sometimes things are absolutely perfect. Everything goes in a direction that can't get any better. Other times things are in such a low that you will feel as though you have no idea how to make them better again. But this is life. This is the challenge of being in a marriage and having to think about more than just yourself.

It can be tempting to use magick to ease your marriage challenges, but any Witch worth her salt knows that it is up to her to do everything she possibly can on the mundane level before calling in the powers of the supernatural.

The God and Goddess will stand by you and support you, as long as you are doing everything humanly possible first. That includes a change in your thinking and attitude. It has been said that we do not pray to change God, but instead to change ourselves. I believe this holds true regardless of the particular faith you practice.

The power of positive thinking is an amazing thing, and has been proven over and over again to be successful in our lives. If we want our marriage to work out, it can. All we have to do is really want it. Unfortunately, a common Pagan attitude concerning handfasting is that if it doesn't work out, no matter what the time frame, we can just go our separate ways and no one is worse off for it. Pagans are not alone in having this attitude toward marriage. But when we make an emotional and sexual commitment to another person, we need to take that commitment seriously. We need to be sure that we want to spend the rest of our lives with that person, not just a year and a day or merely "as long as love shall last." While this is not a rare vow in Pagan circles, it should not be taken to encourage a passive attitude about love. Love is an action, with decision. It is not simply a condition that comes and goes like rain, or even a long-lasting uncontrolled event like the seasons, or climate. Love may start like a summer cloudburst, but it will never live on that way. We must cultivate love with all the will and wisdom we can muster.

The Wiccan Rede says, "True in love ever be, unless thy lover's false to thee." It does not say, "True in love ever be, unless I fall out of love with thee or unless I change my mind about thee, or my lover makes me angry, or I meet an upgrade from thee." It makes no difference if you are a heterosexual, homosexual, transgender, Pagan, or interfaith couple. There are people's emotions and feelings at stake here. Always remember the code of ethics taught to us in the Wiccan Rede: "And it harm none, do what ye will." I have yet to see a handparting that harms none!

To engage in a handfasting is a very serious commitment that should never be taken lightly. Beyond that, it is a promise to the God and Goddess that you will do everything within your power, mundane first and then magickal, to ensure its success. Today it is far too easy to part ways and to forget that you were ever emotionally and spiritually united. I would suggest that, if these words do not ring true for you, you might want to spend some time in introspection and contemplation to figure out exactly why you do not think the word *commitment* is one of the most spiritually important words you will ever speak.

Challenges in Marriage

Marriage is difficult and very challenging, no one is denying that, but "Where there is a Witch there is a way." I can, I will, I believe! If you, as a Pagan, have a sincere spiritual practice that includes a deep spiritual connection with the God and Goddess, then you will understand exactly what I am talking about. If you have not already established such a divine relationship, then I would suggest you develop one, and quickly. Invest time in your own spiritual development. Get yourself to a place where the physical is not more important than the spiritual, but instead equally important. When you have a connection to the God and Goddess, anything is possible, and you will love living with continual inner peace. The connection to the God and Goddess and inner peace are the keys to a successful marriage.

If you are an interfaith couple and your partner is not Pagan, it makes no difference. You already stated in your vows to one another that you would support each other's spiritual beliefs. Hold true to that promise, and encourage your partner to find that comfort and inner peace with her God, too. If your partner is agnostic, then encourage her to find solace in her spirituality, in any way that she can. You will be amazed at how much easier it is to communicate with each other when you are always speaking from a place of love and compassion and inner peace.

Do not rely on your partner for your happiness. Take control of your own life, your own spirituality, your own inner peace, and then share who you are with your partner. Let your partner share in your happiness, but do not expect him to be the source of it. I always say that with expectations comes disappointment. Forget the expectations, and forget the disappointment. Be glad that the God and Goddess have given you a partner with whom to share your life.

Keep the lines of communication always open. Speak from a place of love and compassion, as though the God were sitting on one shoulder and the Goddess on the other. There is no doubt that you would be careful of what you said and how you said it if that were visibly true. But guess what: it is true. The God and Goddess are indwelling in you. They are always with you. Do not turn away from Them. Turn toward Them, and you are sure to have a successful marriage.

Be sure to keep plenty of humor and romance in your marriage. When I was first married to my husband, he would leave for work long before I would get up in the morning. He would leave notes taped to the ceiling that I would see as soon as I awoke. Notes like: "I love you," "Happy one month anniversary," "You're beautiful," and so on. In return, I kept a journal on the kitchen table where I left him love letters and poems, almost on a daily basis. We still write each other love letters and notes fifteen years later. He surprises me with flowers for no reason, and I tell him how wonderful he looks in a suit. The point is not to let the romance end. You can get comfortable with a person, but that is not a reason to take them for granted. It is a reason to affirm why you married that person in the first place.

Remember also that violating a vow does not break a vow. As long as you both intend to keep, or restore, the vows that you made at your handfasting, no violation committed by either or both of you breaks the vow you made. The Rede's reminder to "True in love ever be, unless thy lover's false to thee," is not a free pass to play around because you think your partner is. Nor is it an automatic escape clause. It is a call to fidelity, with the understanding that the sad day could come when it is time for you to move on, provided you have done everything possible, with the help of the God and Goddess, to save the marriage. "True in love ever be," is a call to forgiveness.

It certainly doesn't sound very Wiccan, in many ears, to say that the glorious gift of sex, of marital union, is best expressed between two partners—*you two*—who have committed themselves exclusively and permanently to each other. It almost sounds like a loss of free will. This is so far from the truth! Your free wills, as you grow in your sacred relationship, will find their full-throated voices when you follow the path together, regardless of the path and even its shattering surprises. Sex is wonderful. The Great Rite, however, is sacred. This sacred rite should never be used for anything else: not to control, not to reward, not to manipulate, not to punish. Above all, love and mutual respect is a divine rite that weaves you two lovers together in spirit and in flesh, for all the days of your lives.

Feed and water the blossoms of your love in every way you can. Pluck up the weeds of expectation with the wisdom, swiftness, and compassion that a careful gardener would use in her rose bed. Expectations may even be, like weeds, blossoms that simply need to grow elsewhere. Or they may be best eliminated, like cuttings on a compost pile that find their greatest value when they are gone.

We are Pagans and Witches who relish the metaphysical principles that give real manifestation to our faith, our magick, and our lives. So I'll leave you with an affirmation that when said often and with conviction will ensure that the love, compassion, and security that you find in your first year and a day will only grow stronger as you cultivate it.

"God and Goddess, You are my source of strength and compassion and Your love will forever shine through me as a natural endowment for my loved one. For this I give thanks. And so it is! Blessed be!"

FLOWERS AND THEIR MAGICKAL MESSAGES

White and off-white flowers and herbs and their magickal messages

Acacia The hope of everlasting friendship.

Agapanthus I will shower you with words of love.

Allspice I have a warm heart.

Alyssum Beyond physical beauty.

Amaranth Globe My love is everlasting.

Ambrosia You love me.

Anemone I am truthful and sincere.

Aniseed I am a fountain of youth.

Apple Blossom We have good luck and fortune.

Aster I am pure femininity.

Azalea I have modest passion.

Baby's Breath We share an innocent love.

Calla Lily Full of beauty in elegance.

Camellia I adore you.

Carnation I'm interested in you.

Chamomile We will acquire wealth in time.

Chrysanthemum My Goddess-based Truth.

Daffodil I respect you.

Daisy My love is loyal.

Day Lily I am flirtatious.

Dogwood We have long-lasting love.

Elder I am devoted to you.

Eucalyptus I will protect you.

Feverfew I feel general protection.

Gardenia You are my secret love.

Hyacinth The God and Goddess will keep you safe.

Iris I have faith.

Jasmine You have grace and elegance.

Lily Our relationship is pure.

Magnolia I love all of nature.

Peony I am shy.

Poinsettia Yule tidings.

Primrose You are my soul mate.

Queen Anne's Lace Visions of the Faerie realm.

Rose I will not tell. I will keep all secrets.

Stephanotis We are spiritually united.

Blue flowers and herbs and their magickal messages

Agapanthus I will shower you with words of love.

Aster I am pure femininity.

Forget-Me-Not Don't forget me.

Hyacinth The God and Goddess will keep you safe.

Hydrangea You are so understanding.

Orange or peach flowers and herbs and their magickal messages

Alstroemeria You are my best friend.

Amaryllis I am so proud of you.

Azalea I have modest passion.

Calendula I'm so happy.

Day Lily Our relationship is pure.

Goldenrod We will enjoy the day.

Hibiscus I am petite femininity.

Sunflower We are loyal to each other. Nothing will turn my gaze from you.

Tiger Lily We will be financially successful.

Pink flowers and herbs and their magickal messages

Acanthus (actually mauve and white mixed) I am open to the beauty of artistic expression.

Almond Blossom I'm hopeful our love will last.

Alstroemeria You are my best friend.

Alyssum I see beyond physical beauty.

Amaranth Globe Our love is everlasting.

Azalea I have modest passion.

Bachelor's Buttons I believe in love.

Begonia I am cautious.

Camellia I can't wait to be with you.

Carnation You are unforgettable.

Day Lily Our relationship is pure.

Eucalyptus I am protected by love.

Fuchsia I couldn't have done better.

Heather We have good luck.

Hibiscus I am petite femininity.

Hyacinth The God and Goddess will keep you safe.

Hydrangea You are so understanding.

Mimosa I'm sensitive to your needs.

Morning Glory I love being affectionate.

Orchid You make me feel beautiful.

Peony I am shy.

Rose I am so happy.

Purple flowers and herbs and their magickal messages

Aconite You are my secret love.

Alyssum I see beyond physical beauty.

Aster I am pure femininity.

Bachelor's Buttons I believe in love.

Carnation I'm not afraid of change.

Foxglove I'm whimsical.

Heliotrope I will remain faithful.

Iris I'm wise.

Lavender You are devoted to me.

Lilac You are my one love.

Morning Glory I love being affectionate.

Orchid You make me feel special.

Peony I am shy.

Red flowers and herbs and their magickal messages

Amaranth We will stand still in time.

Amaranth Globe Our love is everlasting.

Amaryllis (red and white) You are intense beauty.

Camellia You are my desire.

Carnation I love you.

Chrysanthemum Forever in love.

Hyacinth The God and Goddess will keep you safe.

Peony I am shy.

Poinsettia Yule tidings.

Tulip Trust my love.

Yellow flowers and herbs and their magickal messages

Broom I am modest.

Buttercup I'm happy like a child.

Calendula I'm so happy.

Carnation You are my friend.

Chrysanthemum You are my best friend.

Daffodil I respect you.

Daisy My love is loyal.

Dandelion My wish has come true.

Elder I am devoted to you.

Hawthorn You give me new hope.

Hyacinth The God and Goddess will keep you safe.

Lily Our relationship is pure.

Primrose I can't live without you.

Rose I care about you.

Tiger Lily We will be financially successful.

Tulip Trust my love.

HERBS AND ESSENTIAL OILS ASSOCIATED WITH LOVE

Alfalfa *(Medicago sativa)*

Alyssum *(Cuneifolium)*

Amber

Apricot *(Prunus armeniaca)*—Do not use the seeds

Aster *(Callistephus chinensis)*

Avocado *(Persea americans)*- Do not use the pit

Bachelor's Buttons *(Centaurea cyanus)*

Balm of Gilead *(Commiphora opobalsmum)*

Banana *(Musa sapientum)*

Barley *(Hordeum spp. vulgare)*

Basil *(Ocimumbasilicum)*

Bedstraw *(Galium verum)*

Benzoin *(Styrax benzoin)*

Caper *(Capparis spinosa)*

Cardamom *(Elettaria caridamomum)*

Catnip *(Nepeta cataria)*

Cattail *(Typha capensis)*

Chickweed *(Stellaria media)*

Cinnamon *(Cinnamomum zeylanicum)*

Columbine *(Aquilegia canadensis)*—Do not use the seeds

Copal *(Bursera odorata)*

Cuckoo *(Orchis morior)*

Damiana *(Turnera diffuse)*

Devil's Bit *(Scabiosa succisa)*

Dill *(Anethum graveolens)*

Dragon's Blood *(Daemonorops draco)*

Elm *(Ulmus campestris)*

Endive *(Cichorium endivia)*

Eryngo *(Eryngium spp. maritinum)*

Frankincense *(Boswellia carterii)*

Gardenia *(Gardenia jasminoides)*

Ginger *(Zingiber officinale)*

Hibiscus *(Hibiscus spp. sabdariffa)*

Lady's Mantle *(Alchemilla vulgaris)*

Lavender *(Lavendula officinale)*

Lemon *(Citrus limon)*

Lemon Balm *(Melissa officinalis)*

Lemon Verbena *(Lippia citriodora)*

Love Seed *(Lomatium foeniculaceum)*

Mallow *(Malva sylvestris)*

Maple *(Acer spp.)*

Marjoram *(Origanum majorana)*

Meadow Rue *(Tahlictrum spp.)*

Meadowsweet *(Spiraea filipendula)*

Mimosa *(Acacia dealbeta)*

Mistletoe *(Viscum album)*—Do not use the American variety

Moonwort *(Botrychium spp.)*

Myrrh *(Commiophora myrrha)*

Orchid *(Orchis spp.)*

Orris powder *(Iris germanica var. florentina)*

Pansy *(Viola tricolor)*

Patchouly *(Pogostemon cablin)*

Peach *(Prunus persica)*—Do not use the seed, leaf, or bark

Pear *(Pyrus communis)*—Do not use the seed

Poppy *(Papaver spp.)*

Prickly Ash *(Zanthoxylum americanum)*—Do not use the bark

Primrose *(Primula vulgaris)*—Be careful using on skin

Quassia *(Picraena excelsa)*

Raspberry *(Rubus idaeus)*

Red Sandalwood *(Pterocarpus santalinus)*

Rose *(Rosa spp.)*—Anything green is poisonous

Rosemary *(Rosemarinus officinalis)*

Skullcap *(Scutellatia lateriflora)*

Senna *(Cassia marilandica)*

Strawberry *(Fagaria vesca)*

Tea leaves *(Camellia sinensis)*

Thyme *(Thymus vulgaris)*

Tormentil *(Potentilla erecta)*

Trillium *(Trillium spp. erectum)*

Tulip *(Tulipa spp.)*

Vanilla *(Vanilla aromatica)*

Violet *(Viola odorata)*

Willow *(Salix alba)*

Witch Grass *(Agropyron repens)*

BIBLIOGRAPHY

Adler, Margot. *Drawing Down the Moon*. New York: Penguin Group, 2006.

Ali, Maulana Muhammad. *The Holy Qur'an with commentaries by Maulana Muhammad Ali*. Dublin, OH: Ahmadiyya Anjuman Isha'at Islam Lahore Inc., 2002.

Baldizzoni, Gianni, and Tiziana Baldizzoni. *Wedding Ceremonies: Ethnic Symbols, Costume, and Rituals*. New York: Flammarion Press, 2002.

Barrett, Bruce. Personal Interview. January 7, 2007.

Budd, Eric Merrill. *Scottish Tartan Weddings: A Practical Guidebook*. New York: Hippocrene Books, 1999.

Conway, D.J. *Magick of the Gods and Goddesses*. Berkeley, CA: The Crossing Press, 2003.

Cunningham, Scott. *Complete Book of Incense, Oils, and Brews*. St. Paul, MN: Llewellyn, 2002.

_____. *Cunningham's Encyclopedia of Magical Herbs*. St. Paul, MN: Llewellyn, 2000.

Davies, Elizabeth. "A Brief History of the Wedding Dress in Britain." E2davies.net. *http://www.geocities.com/e2davies/brides.html* (accessed December 2006).

Delamore, Philip. *The Perfect Wedding Dress*. Toronto: Firefly Books, 2006.

Field, Ann and Gretchen Scoble. *The Meaning of Flowers*. San Francisco: Chronicle Books, 1998.

Friend, Pat. "Handfasting: An Ancient Irish Wedding Tradition." *http://www.handfasting.info/histirish.html* (accessed December 2006).

Gies, Frances and Joseph. *Marriage and the Family in the Middle Ages*, reprint edition. New York: Harper Perennial, 1989.

Goldentree Wands. "Color Magick." *http://goldentreewands.com/colormagic.htm* (accessed May 2007).

Guilbault, Melody and Julianne. *Love Is in the Earth: A Kaleidoscope of Crystals*. Wheat Ridge, CO: Earth-Love Publishing House, Ltd., 1995.

Kaplan-Mayer, Gabrielle. *The Creative Jewish Wedding Book*. Woodstock, VT: Jewish Lights Publishing, 2004.

Kiefer, Otto. *Sexual Life in Ancient Rome*. Whitefish, MT: Kessinger, 2003.

Krossa, Sharon L. "Historical Handfasting." *http://www.medievalscotland.org/history/handfasting.shtml* (accessed December 2006).

LoveToKnow Corp. "History of Wedding Flowers." *http://weddings.lovetoknow.com/wiki/History_of_Wedding_Flowers* (accessed December 2006).

Macomb, Susanna Stefanachi. *Joining Hands and Hearts: Interfaith, Intercultural Wedding Celebrations: A Practical Guide for Couples*. New York: Atria, 2002.

Muchnick, Cynthia Clumeck. *The Ultimate Wedding Idea Book: 1,001 Creative Ideas to Make Your Wedding Fun, Romantic, and Memorable*. Roseville, CA: Three Rivers Press, 2001.

Pandya, Meenal Atul. *Vivah: Design a Perfect Hindu Wedding*. Wellesley, MA: MeeRa Publications, 2000.

RavenWolf, Silver. *Solitary Witch*. St. Paul, MN: Llewellyn Publications, 2003.

Reade, W. Winwood. "The Veil of Isis; or, Mysteries of the Druids." Internet Sacred Text Archive. *http://www.sacred-texts.com/pag/motd/motd.htm* (accessed May 2007).

Sacred Sanctuary Blog. *http://p088.ezboard.com/Handfasting/fsacred sanctuaryfrm20.showMessage?topicID=98.topic* (accessed May 2007).

Spangenberg, Lisl M. *Timeless Traditions: A Couple's Guide to Wedding Customs Around the World*. New York: Universe Publications, 2001.

Stewart, Arlene Hamilton. *A Bride's Book of Wedding Traditions*. New York: William Morrow, 1995.

Sullivan III, C.W. "'Jumping the Broom': A Further Consideration of the Origins of an African American Wedding Custom." The Questia Online Library. *http://www.questia.com/PM.qst?a=o&se=gglsc&d=96464500* (accessed May 2007).

Telesco, Patricia. *Gardening with the Goddess*. Franklin Lakes, NJ: New Page Books, 2001.

Waggoner, Susan. *I Do! I Do!: From the Veil to the Vows: How Classic Wedding Traditions Came to Be*. New York: Rizzoli International Publications, 2002.

Weddings.co.uk. "Wedding Superstitions & Traditions." *http://www.weddings.co.uk/info/tradsup.htm* (accessed May 2007).

Westermarck, Edward Alexander. *The History of Human Marriage*. Chestnut Hill, MA: Adamant Media Corporation, 2000.

Wikipedia. "Aengus." Wikimedia Foundation, Inc. *http://en.wikipedia.org/wiki/Aengus* (accessed December 2006).

_____. "List of Jewish prayers and blessings." Wikimedia Foundation, Inc. *http://en.wikipedia.org/wiki/List_of_Jewish_prayers_and_blessings* (accessed December 2006).

_____. "Wedding Dress." Wikimedia Foundation, Inc. *http://en.wikipedia.org/wiki/Wedding_dress* (accessed December 2006).

Yogananda, Paramahansa. *The Bhagavad Gita with commentaries by Paramahansa Yogananda.* Los Angeles: Self-Realization Fellowship, 2001.

Ziglar, Zig. "Healthy Fear." Evan Carmichael. *http://www.evancarmichael.com/Entrepreneur-Advice/448/Healthy-Fear.html* (accessed May 2007).

Zimmermann, Denise, and Katherine A. Gleason. *The Complete Idiot's Guide to Wicca and Witchcraft.* New York: Penguin Group, 2006.

Zondervan. *NIV Study Bible.* Grand Rapids, MI: Zondervan, 2002.

INDEX